ARTS/SCIENCES: ALLOYS

The Thesis Defense of
IANNIS XENAKIS

Iannis Xenakis

Mariecke Benetti 1983

ARTS/SCIENCES: ALLOYS

The Thesis Defense of
IANNIS XENAKIS

before

Olivier Messiaen, Michel Ragon
Olivier Revault d'Allonnes, Michel Serres,
and Bernard Teyssèdre

Translated by Sharon Kanach

AESTHETICS IN MUSIC No. 2

Pendragon Press New York, N.Y.

Aesthetics in Music Series

No. 1   *Analysis and Value Judgment* by Carl Dahlhaus,
         Translated by Siegmund Levarie (1983)
         ISBN 0-918728-20-7

No. 3   *Divining the Powers of Music: Aesthetic Theory
         and the Origins of Opera* by Ruth Katz (in press)

Other Pendragon Press Musicological Series:

The Sociology of Music
French Opera in the 17th & 18th Centuries
Monographs in Musicology
The Juilliard Performance Guides
The Historical Harpsichord
Thematic Catalogues

RILM Retrospectives
Annotated Reference Tools in Music
Festschrift Series

Library of Congress Cataloging in Publication Data

Xenakis, Iannis, 1922–
   Arts-sciences alloys.

   (Pendragon Press aesthetics in music series: no. 2)
   Translation of: Arts-sciences alliages.
   1. Music–Philosophy and aesthetics. 2. Art and
science. I. Messiaen, Olivier, 1908–   .
II. Title.   III. Series.
ML3800.X3813   1985   780'.1   82-11261
ISBN 0-918728-22-3

220786

Originally Published by:
Editions Casterman, s.a.
28, rue des Soeurs Noires
Tournai, Belgium
(1979)

780.1
Xen

CONTENTS

v

AUTHOR'S PREFACE

In France, the "Doctorat d'Etat" may be awarded on the basis of a "file" consisting of previously published theoretical and creative works. This thesis file must then be defended before a jury whose members (not necessarily academic personalities) are suggested to the sponsoring university by the candidate. Once all the members have been agreed upon, a five-hour deliberation session is held between the candidate and the jury. At the end of this "defense," the jury decides whether the degree should be awarded, and if so, with what honors. The present volume is a translation of the defense of the material in my file which was recorded at the Sorbonne in 1976.

I am very proud to have had the chance to debate the issues covered in this volume with this distinguished company. Many of these subjects have preoccupied me since my youth, and it was an honor to discuss them with the specialists on the jury, each of them being part of the French intellectual avant-garde in his domain.

I admire the perseverance, courage, and intelligence of the young composer Sharon Kanach, first for having translated this book and, second, for finding Pendragon Press, an American publishing house that was willing to bring out a work which guaranteed no particular commercial success. Through the innocence of her youth and her love for these same subjects, Sharon fought through the problems of publication, mostly on her own. I would like to express my gratitude to Sharon and to Robert Kessler of Pendragon Press.

Iannis Xenakis

TRANSLATOR'S PREFACE

The text of *Arts/Sciences:Alloys* is a transcription made from the tape recordings of Xenakis' thesis defense for a "doctorat d'Etat" at the Sorbonne in the spring of 1976. In this translation, I have tried to render the written word as close to "speech" as possible while not betraying the grammatical logic behind the statements. French and English *verbal* patterns differ greatly, and I have tried to make them coincide in *written* expression with the intention of avoiding the impression of a translation *per se*.

A note of thanks is due first of all to Iannis Xenakis himself for initially suggesting this translation to me. His encouragement, help, and meticulous attention throughout the years and especially during this project have been very valuable and are most appreciated.

My gratitude goes to Cornelia Coyler of CEMAMu* for her efficient cooperation in putting essential materials at my disposal.

Deep thanks to Robert Pépin for his patience and thoughtful eye, ear, and translation experience and friendship throughout the various phases of this undertaking.

*CEMAMu: Centre d'Etudes de Mathematiques et Automatique Musicales; in other words, Xenakis' Computer Studio, housing the "UPIC" computer, designed by the composer which functions as a sort of "musical drawing board." This machine renders direct music making accessible to everyone. Workshops have been held with children, handicapped people (including the blind) as well as musicians, architects, etc. The studio is housed in the suburbs of Paris in the French National Center for Studies in Telecommunications (CNET). (Trans. note)

A special note of thanks must also go to Robert Kessler, who first recognized the importance of an English language edition of this book and without whom it would not now exist.

Finally, I would like to dedicate this translation to my parents, Elizabeth and Walter Kanach.

Sharon E. Kanach

NOTICE

This is a transcription of Iannis Xenakis' thesis defense which took place on May 18, 1976 at the Sorbonne (Paris). Presiding over the jury was Bernard Teyssèdre, professor of aesthetics at the University of Paris-Sorbonne. Jury members were: Olivier Messiaen, professor at the National Conservatory of Music; Michel Ragon, professor at the National School of Decorative Arts; Olivier Revault d'Allonnes, professor at the University of Paris-Sorbonne (thesis director and advisor); and Michel Serres, professor at the University of Paris-Sorbonne.

List of Illustrations

$$\nearrow | \nwarrow$$

PRELIMINARY STATEMENT
BY IANNIS XENAKIS

Subtended Philosophy*

The worlds of classical, contemporary, pop, folk, traditional, avant-garde, etc., music seem to form unities unto themselves; sometimes closed, sometimes intersecting. Not only do they present extraordinary deviations, rich in new creations, but also fossilizations, ruins, and wastes, all in continuous formations and transformations, much like clouds—so distinct yet so ephemeral.

This can be explained by the proposition that music is a sociocultural phenomenon; therefore, subordinate to a given moment in history. Yet we can distinguish the parts which are more invariable than others and which then form materials of hardness and consistency resulting from various epochs of civilization; materials which move in space, have been developed, put into use, and have followed the course of ideas, colliding one against the other, influencing and annihilating one another, mutually fecundating.

But what is the essence of these materials? This essence is man's intelligence, in some way solidified. Intelligence which searches, questions, infers, reveals, foresees—on all levels. Music and the arts in general seem to be a necessary solidification, materialization of this intelligence. Naturally, intelligence, although humanly universal, is diversified by the individual, by talent, which distinguishes one individual from others.

*An excerpt of this text has been published in *Musique, Architecture*, pp. 181-87, in the collection "Syntheses contemporaines," Paris, Editions Casterman 1976.

Talent, then, is a kind of qualification, a grading of the vigor and richness of intelligence; for intelligence is, fundamentally, the result or expression of the billions of exchanges, reactions and energy transformations of the body and the brain cells. Using the model of astrophysics, we could say that intelligence is the form which minimal acts take in cellular condensations and movements— as it seems to be with solar, planetary and galactic movements, and in galactic constellations, born of or reduced to cold interstellar dust. However, this image is inverted (at least on one level), for in condensation, this cold dust becomes hot, contrary to intelligence which is cold, "a cold fire," resulting from the exchanges between the hot cells of the brain and body.

Therefore, colors, sounds and dimensions are condensations in our sensory-brain system. A brutal and perfectly superficial exterior aspect of this system is perceived and comprehended on the conscious level. The periodic vibrations in the air and the electromagnetic field of light are inaccessible to the conscience but are magnificently well followed (within limits, of course) and converted by our senses and brain. One's senses are the extension of the brain. Conversions, on the other hand, operate on several levels, from that of immediate perception to those of comparison, appreciation and judgment. How, why is all of this produced? It is a mystery, elaborated as it is among the animals, and this has been so for millions and millions of years.

All the same, let's take an example which appears to be relatively obvious, that of musical scales. There have been, at least in the Western world, stronger and stronger condensations: the perfect fourth and tetrachords, and perhaps even earlier, the perfect fifth (whose origins remain unknown); then, the octave, followed by the construction of "systems" by tetrachordal juxtapositions that had engendered Antiquity's scales, from which the diatonic scale of white keys on the keyboard is one survivor. Next came the evenly tempered chromatic scale, and finally, continuity in the ensemble of "pitches."

It follows from this example that music is a strong condenser, the strongest, perhaps, of all the arts. This is why I am giving a comparative table* between certain conquests achieved by music

*See *Musique. Architecture*, Annex 1, pp. 192–96, and Appendix I, p. 00 of present volume.

2

and several mathematical realizations such as history teaches us. This table shows one of the paths music has taken since its origin (since Antiquity) and to which it has kept with remarkable fidelity through millennia, marking a significant acceleration during the twentieth century. This proves that the faculty of condensation-toward-abstraction is part of music's profound nature (more than any other art's) rather than simply being a function. Consequently, it seems that a new type of musician is necessary, an "artist-conceptor" of new abstract and free forms, tending toward complexities, and then toward generalizations on several levels of sound organization. For example, a form, a construction, an organization based on Markov chains or on a complex of interrelated probablitiy functions can be simultaneously conveyed on several levels of musical micro-, meso-, and macro-composition. We could even extend this concept to the visual domain, for example, in a *spectacle* involving laser rays and electronic flashes such as those of the *Cluny Polytope.* *

From here on nothing prevents us from foreseeing a new relationship between the arts and sciences, especially between the arts and mathematics; where the arts would consciously "set" problems which mathematics would then be obliged to solve through the invention of new theories.

The artist-conceptor will have to be knowledgeable and inventive in such varied domains as mathematics, logic, physics, chemistry, biology, genetics, paleontology (for the evolution of forms), the human sciences and history; in short, a sort of universality, but one based upon, guided by and oriented toward forms and architectures. Moreover, the time has come to establish a new science of "general morphology" which would treat these forms and architectures within these diverse disciplines in their invariant aspects and the laws of their transformations which have, in some cases, existed for millions of years. The backdrop for this new science should be the real condensations of intelligence; in other words, an abstract approach, free from anecdotes of our senses and habits.

Let us now delve into the fundamental system on which art

---

*Also, the Diatope at the Georges Pompidou Arts Center, cf. fn. p. 52 of present volume (trans. note). For further description, see listings in Catalogue of Works.

is based. Art has something in the nature of an inferential mechanism which constitutes the platforms on which all theories of the mathematical, physical and human sciences move about. Indeed, games of proportion—reducible to number games and metrics in architecture, literature, music, painting, theatre, dance, etc., games of continuity, of proximity, in or outside of time, topological essence—all occur on the terrain of *inference*, in the strict, logical sense of the word. Situated next to this terrain and operating in reciprocal activity is the *experimental mode* which challenges or confirms theories created by the sciences, including mathematics. Mathematics, ever since non-Euclidian geometry and theorems such as Gödel's, has proven itself experimental, but in a wider sense than is applicable to the other sciences. It is experimentation which makes or breaks theories, pitilessly and without any particular consideration for the theories themselves. Yet the arts are governed in a manner even richer and more complex by this experimental mode. Certainly there is not nor will there ever be an objective criterion for determining absolute truth or eternal validity even within one work of art, just as no scientific "truth" is ever definitive. But in addition to these two modes—inferential and experimental—art exists in a third mode, one of immediate *revelation*, which is neither inferential nor experimental. The revelation of beauty occurs immediately, directly, to someone ignorant of art as well as to the connoisseur. This is the strength of art and, so it seems, its superiority over the sciences. Art, while living the two dimensions of inference and experimentation, possesses this third and most mysterious dimension which permits art objects to escape any aesthetic science while still enjoying the caresses of inference and experimentation.

But on the other hand, art cannot live by the revelation mode alone. Art history of all times and of all civilizations shows us that art has an imperious need of organization (including that of chance); therefore, a need for inference and its confirmation; hence, a need for its experimental truth.

To shed some light on this trinity of modes in art, let's imagine that in a distant future, the power of artistic action will increase as it never before has in history (which has been humanity's path in the development and dissipation of the quantities of energy growth). Actually there is no reason why art cannot, following the example of science, rise from the immensity of the cosmos; nor why art cannot, as a cosmic landscaper, modify the demeanor of the galaxies.

This may seem utopian, and in fact it is, but only temporarily when viewed in the context of the immensity of time. On the contrary, what is not utopian but possible today is to cast luminous spiderwebs of colored laser beams like a giant polytope over cities and countrysides: the use of clouds as reflector screens, the use of artificial satellites as reflecting mirrors so that these "webs" rise in space and surround the earth with their phantasmagorical, moving geometrics; joining the earth and the moon by filaments of light. One could even willfully create artificial aurora boreales in the night skies whose movements, forms and colors would be controlled by electromagnetic fields aroused by lasers in the highest atmosphere. As for music, loudspeaker technology is still at the embryonic stage, too underdeveloped to send sound into space and have it received there, in thunder's home.

But hedgehopping sound displacements in cities and over the countryside are already possible thanks to national networks of air raid alarm system speakers. It would suffice to merely refine them.*

If countries' economies were not tortured by strategic and armament needs—in other words, on the day when the nation's armies would diminish into simple, non-repressive police forces—then, financially, art could fly over our planet and soar into the cosmos. Technologically speaking, these things are feasible today.

In these planetary or cosmic artistic productions, it is apparent that the artist, and consequently art, must be simultaneously

---

* I have already presented two of these ideas as project proposals:

1) To install a laser network over Paris joining the highest points in the city in an interplay with the clouds while broadcasting a specific music through the loudspeakers of the air raid sirens. This project was conceived for the inauguration of the Georges Pompidou Center.

2) A network of laser beams to be reflected by artificial satellites, joining the continents at precise points situated near significant agglomerations where the local polytope centers, open to the general public, could react between one another (intercontinentally), following pre-established game rules similar to those in my musical game piece for two conductors and two orchestras, *Strategie*, or those of *Linaia-Agon*.

Both projects were rejected because of the implied expenses though both are technically feasible.

rational (inferential), technical (experimental) and talented (reve-latory); three indispensable and coordinated modes which shun fatal failures, given the dimensions of these projects and the great risk of error.

This greater complexity of the fundamental system of the three modes which govern art leads to the conclusion that art is richer and vaster and must necessarily initiate condensations and coagulations of intelligence; therefore, serve as a universal guide to the other sciences.

COAGULATIONS

For more than twenty years now, I have strived like a mosaic artisan, unconsciously at first, then in a more conscious way, to fill this philosophical space with an intelligence which becomes real by the colored pebbles which are my musical, architectural and visual works and my writings. These pebbles, at first very isolated, have found themselves brought together by bonds of relationships, of affinities, but also by opposition, gradually forming figures of local coherencies and then vaster fields summon-ing each other with questions and then the resulting answers. Mathematics plays an essential role here as a philosophical cata-lyst, as a molding tool for forming auditory or visual edifices, but also as a springboard toward self-liberation. Here I will outline only the fundamental questions and, in opposition to these, the answers given by the works I have created. I will not, in any case, go into detail nor explain the mazes of their elaboration. Further-more, several of these questions are interrelated and create inter-sections belonging to the same philosophical domain. For example: causality—determinism—continuity, indeterminism (chance)—exis-tentiality—determinism, etc. This is also why a work (answer) can, in itself, respond to a whole group of questions. It's a bit like be-ing in the presence of sound-as-questions, rich in harmonics and considering one or another harmonic as being the fundamental, following the quest at a given moment.

In addition, I will mention only a few works from the thesis file.*

Questions	Answers
existentiality	ST/10-1, 080262
in-time, outside-time	Nomos gamma
causality	ST/10-1, 080262, Nomos gamma Tourette Convent (facades), repetition or or not of modules.
inference	Nomos gamma, ST/10-1, 080262
connectedness	Empreintes (aborescences), Metastasis (glissandi forms) Philips Pavillon (shell, line forms)
compacity	Metastasis, Philips Pavillon, Nomos gamma
impure determinism	Strategie, Syrmos, game theory Markov chains
pure determinism	Nomos gamma (groups)
identity (similitude, equivalence)	All works

The visual theatrics of the *Polytopes*** deal with questions and answers musically set and resolved, but here with lasers, electronic flashes and in space. What is remarkable to ascertain is that these questions can be found in all areas of musical or visual composition; in other words, from the general form (macrocomposition) down to computer-generated sound synthesis and numeric-analogical conversion (microcomposition), but also passing by all the intermediary stages along the way. "The paths from both the top and bottom make but one."

I was saying that all the work I have done over the years is a sort of mosaic of hierarchical coherencies. At the hierarchy's summit I'd place philosophy.

---

*Xenakis, for the "Doctorat d'Etat, presented his entire creative and theoretical output to date, rather than write a dissertation on a specific subject. This collection of works constituted his "thesis file." (trans. note)
**Cf. above, p. 3 plus Catalogue of Works, p. 117 of present volume. (trans. note)

Philosophy, but in what sense? In the sense of the philosophical impulse which pushes us toward truth, revelation, research, general quest, interrogation, and harsh systematic criticism, not only in specialized fields but in all possible domains. This leads us to an ensemble of knowledge which should be active, in the sense of "doing." Not passive knowledge but knowledge which is translated into creative acts. I repeat, in all possible domains.

Following the methods which I will examine presently, one can divide this coherency roster, mosaic, this table, into three categories or three chapters. The first is the method which allows us to obtain this active knowledge through creativity—which (through theoretical demonstration) implies inference, meaning reason, logic, etc. Following these criteria, there are aspects of activity and knowledge which are partially inferential, entirely inferential and experimental, and others which remain unknown.

I'd put the arts in the "partially inferential" region. The arts take part in inference. Consequently, we construct and tie things together in a reasoned manner and can demonstrate them up to a certain point. On the contrary, the human and natural sciences, physics, mathematics, and logic are experimental as well as entirely inferential. It is necessary to build a theory and to verify this theory by experimentation. In the artistic domain, we can partially build by inference, but experimentation is not immediate. There is the problem of aesthetics and there is no possible demonstration of the aesthetic value of these things. I will leave the door open to any methods which have not yet been discovered.

As a corollary to this artistic discrimination, it can be said that the arts are freer since the arts take part in the inferential operation as well as in the experimental one. It is perhaps ambitious to say it, but the arts could possibly guide other sectors of human thinking. In other words, I would place the arts at the head of man's activities in such a manner that they would seep through *all* of his daily life.

Going down one rung in this hierarchy, I'd say that after this, there is a category of questions which can be asked, questions which have been dodged by history and which can be rediscovered and asked anew: meaning a sort of creatively philosophical fragmenting of directions. Within these categories, there is existentiality (ontology, reality), causality, contiguity or connectedness, compacity, temporal or spacial ubiquity, even inference, all taken as consequences from potentially new mental structures. There is also determinism and its extreme pole, indeterminism. I am reaching back, in one way or another, to certain very important categories of thought which have been more or less consciously and systematically stated since Aristotle but which have drifted by the wayside or been claimed by experimental psychology (Jean Piaget) and certain branches of modern mathematics.

These categories of thought-questions invite or could invite families of solutions and this is what I have endeavored to achieve musically. I hope I am being clear. What I am trying to say is that man has attempted to answer this multitude of questions by giving temporary answers from certain families of solutions, especially with regard to determinism.

Here I would like to open a parenthesis: causality, for example, is one form experienced in life which refers to this fundamental question of determinism (which itself can be considered a nuanced differential aspect of indeterminism). Something I neglected to state before is that it can even be ascertained that order and disorder are parts of indeterminism. Connectedness and continuity are other facets of the bi-pole of determinism-indeterminism.

Picking up where I left off before, solutions and procedures capable of giving answers to categories of fundamental questions are necessarily defined in a very schematic manner by a few sub-chapters, a few paragraphs. Probabilistic thinking—with its extreme limit which I will call free or memory-less stochastics on the one hand, and Markov chains which agree to a certain degree of causality, a certain elementary determinism (which is upstream from this) on the other hand—is one example. But at the heart of probabilistic thinking and indeterminism, there is what can be called symmetry or periodicity, which is another way to define or to speak of these types of thinking. Symmetry or periodicity, meaning the cyclic return of events, procedures, etc., can coagulate through group structures at the bottom of the determinism scale. Between the two, there is what can be called the hybrid or mixed phase. One of the interesting forms in this phase is game theory. Lower, at the lowest threshold of the mosaic, in answer to these topics and ways of thinking (which have also been established by other sciences, including music) specific works can be found which are reflections on and tentative answers to these questions. I don't want to enumerate them here, for that would be too tedious. But I could say, for example, that

9

the topic of free stochastics is treated in a piece such as *Achor-ripsis*, which was later formulated by a machine program, a program which represents a free stochastic *system*. This program made it possible to write works such as *ST/10, ST/48* for orchestra, but also to enter the realm of sonic microstructures and computer-generated sound synthesis. By the way, this same program has been in use for the past few years in the United States as well as in Europe (Sweden, France, etc.), in studios other than CEMAMu,* as well as by other composers. In the realm of Markovian stochastics, there are pieces such as *Analogiques* and *Syrmos* for strings. In game theory: *Strategie, Linaia-Agon*, etc.

From symmetrical/periodical systems, there is *Akrata, Nomos Alpha, Nomos Gamma,* and *Persephassa*, works composed on group structures. I am mentioning only the principal works. In the report I submitted to the jury, and at the beginning of my statement, a few more details can be found which concern my visual works such as the *Polytopes* and my architectural works.

By continuing in this manner down to the very bottom of the hierarchy, one finds the pressure-time space of sound. Analogous things could be said about the visual realm, meaning that from the questions asked on the microstructural level (that is to say, from the level of the next higher element), macrostructures can be seen as resolved or as being treated by procedures and thoughts equivalent on the primordial level. At this primordial level, we find pressure in function with time for the ear and in function with electromagnetic actions for the eye in the visible spectrum. We can summarize by saying that all which has been drawn from the macrostructures' most general fundamental problems is duplicated on all of the elementary structural levels within medio-structures, meso-structures, all the way down the scale which intermingles with quantic action, as I call it, dealing with the two senses of vision and hearing.

I believe I have given you a very general outline of the binding thread throughout my work, without speaking of the work itself.

---

*cf. p. ix for description of CEMAMu (trans.)

10

DIALOGUE WITH
OLIVIER REVAULT D'ALLONES

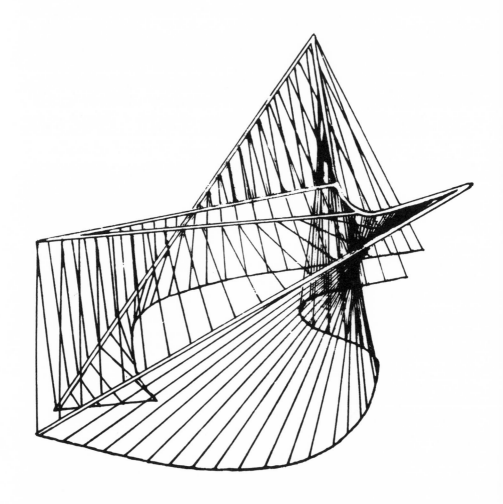

Fig. 1.   The 1954 International Exposition in Brussels.
First model of the Philips Pavilion.

BERNARD TEYSSÈDRE

Thank you very much, Iannis Xenakis. It is certain that your statement was brief and could seem complex since it is so dense. I hope that the discussion which will now get under way will throw some light upon your presentation. It is quite unambiguous for those who already know your work well. But your presentation may seem a bit vague to others, precisely because too many subjects were broached simultaneously. I believe that Revault d'Allonnes, your thesis advisor, could intervene at this point.

OLIVIER REVAULT D'ALLONNES

Indeed, because of some administrative peculiarity, I am the thesis advisor. In reality, Iannis Xenakis' thesis advisor is Iannis Xenakis himself. He managed that well. I am also the chairman of the jury for this defense. Faced with such a considerable mass of research and works, this chairman feels pretty insignificant. What I believe I can be is a spectator among others, and a spectator fascinated by the whole of Xenakis' work.

Xenakis has chosen a title to present his fundamental theoretical works and, in support of these theoretical works, a certain number of documents which are the musical scores of some of the works he just referred to, plus architectural sketches, designs, schemas, abstracts, etc. This general titles defines not only this file, but also the whole of Xenakis' artistic output: *Arts/Sciences: Alloys*. Xenakis introduces a few of these alloys, and has just told us, in a very dense manner, how we can gain insight into these.

"Art," as understood by Xenakis, refers to the latin *artifex*, the creative inventor. This man has a certain attitude before the world, a certain vision of the world, and he feels the permanent and haunting obsession that there is always something to do. For nearly twenty years, I have never seen him other than as prey to a sort of creative demon. For him, science is something which

13

always accompanies this creative demon. Xenakis wants to do something, but not just anything. He always wants to compose a determined work, a work which, on a certain level (precisely on the aesthetic level) communicates itself: you go to a concert, you hear a piece by Xenakis; but the work, on another level, can be communicated in another way, by an analytical, rational language which simultaneously analyzes and justifies this work.

In books such as those he presents today: *Musique. Architecture.* and perhaps especially *Formalized Music,** we see that works are analyzed, decorticated, and at the same time, they are justified, legitimized. Xenakis says why he wanted to do this and how he did it, but the "why" is at least as important as the "how." These "alloys" are indeed not without problems, for me at least. They are architectural and musical works, the polytopes, but also included is the theoretical work we have before our eyes. I would now like to invite those more competent than myself to carefully reflect on art and science and to ask Xenakis questions concerning the "alloys."

The first question will be as follows: Xenakis proposes in his theoretical works to fight against the current separation between the arts and the sciences and to create a sort of free movement of thought; hence a mutually fecundating of scientific and artistic thought. To achieve this, Xenakis relies simultaneously on a vision of the past and on his current realizations. Little by little, we see a vision of the past reappear in each of his works and even in the presentation he has just given. The best periods of mutual fecundating between the arts and the sciences have been during Greek Antiquity, the Italian Renaissance, the classic age, etc., when artists and scholars ignored each other less than they do today and from whence an entirely legitimate nostalgia is born for this free movement between art and science.

But today, the benefits which the arts and sciences could share seem to me to be quite unequally divided and possible. I'm under the impression that the sciences can bring infinitely more services, more illuminations, more fecundations to the arts, and particularly to music, than music can bring to scientific knowledge. For example, the application of stochastic calculations to music, including the sieve theory** which Xenakis personally tailored to apply to the problem of pitch scales is, in essence, as

*See Catalogue of Works, p. 125.
**cf. Appendix II, p. 103.

he says in the first part of *Musique. Architecture.*, for the renewal of music and musicology. But from a purely mathematical point of view, I fear that these tools neither present any particular interest nor fecundity nor invention nor difficulty to surmount, and, by consequence, there is no new realization to be made. Likewise, the use of computers has certainly posed problems, but entirely classical problems in terms of programming and information theory. In short, problems which have been mastered perfectly enough. This is not at all apparent in the other direction. Today, it can be said (and a large part of Xenakis' output has proven) that musical thinking has not yet sufficiently utilized all the mathematical resources it could. When Xenakis realized that for a musician, pitch scales constitute a well-ordered group, an abelian scale, (a trivial definition for a mathematician's mind), this put the "bug in his ear," as they say. There are well-ordered groups; therefore, perhaps there are groups that are not orderly. Here's an abelian scale, can't there be a scale which is not? We understand very well how musical thought can thereby be fertilized by mathematics, but given the relatively elementary level of mathematics in these concepts, I would say that the interest is null for mathematics. If one can dream of an exchange between the arts and the sciences, it would consequently be necessary to declare that, in our day and age, the terms of exchange seem extremely unequal. Hence my question: How can we hope to interest the scholars and scientists and thereby perceive these new mental structures which Xenakis himself alludes to today? Art's use of science benefits the former more than the latter. Is this lack of balance bad? And if yes, how can we overcome this?

My second question is simply derived from the first. The position of free movement and alloys is but a proposition—meaning it doesn't refer to any real situation today; it is a desired state. An alloy is a utopian thing, meaning that it is a creative invention. It is created, so to speak, by the fecundity of Xenakis' work. But can it pretend to apply to the whole of society? Can it pretend to become if not the sole law, at least one of the elements in the relationship between art and science? Would the proposition of "alloys," assuming science to be on one side and art on the other, have something which resembles a meaning-unto-itself, a sort of truth-in-itself; or, with art on its *own* side and science on *its* own side, could they not be vehicles of something other than themselves? Would they stem from somewhere else, a somewhere which

15

would be elsewhere than in the axiomatics to which we enjoy referring them? In other words, is there a purely technical union between the arts and sciences, or is there a social division after all which would be hiding behind this technical division (and if so, which)? Here, I'm not particularly thinking of a class difference between intellectuals and laborers. Indeed, who would be who and who would not? Here we are faced with a division, a separation between functions. Science is turned toward so-called rational action, toward nature and man; it prides itself on being part of reality. Art is turned toward the creative invention of imaginary objects. Is Xenakis proposing something imminently realizable or something which presupposes transformations—notably social ones which are much more radical—by partially changing both science and art, in having them confront one another?

In summary, the sciences have given men a certain control over things. Xenakis now proposes, in some way, to control this control so that this higher control could help man rather than use him. Therefore, is it conceivable that this reversal of terms which circulates throughout Xenakis' entire *oeuvre* limits itself exclusively to the realm of the arts and sciences?

The third question will come back to aesthetics. The opinion is, alas, very widespread that Xenakis' music is composed by computers. This opinion is but one of the aspects of the well-known scientific and technocratic ideology in society. When we look more carefully we can see that this obviously has no meaning. In *Formalized Music* we can find an admirable formula: "In this domain we find that computers render certain services." In other words, it is possible that one may not benefit from these "services." This was the case with *Metastasis* in 1954, and I can still see Xenakis calculating "by hand" (as he said) with incredible patience, no, obstinacy, taking several months to do what a computer could achieve in a few hours. Fine. We have here then months of hard work: If possible, we would use a machine which could work much faster and more efficiently. There are works from Xenakis' more recent output which were also calculated "by hand," works which we could call "hand-crafted," without the use of computers. Perhaps Xenakis can tell us why? I'm thinking of such works as *Nuits*, for example, from 1967 and more recently, *Evryali*, from the summer of 1973. I've been trying to analyze these scores for over two years now. It is not true that these works are the least interesting (at least for my taste); I was going to say in terms of beauty, but let's say in terms of aesthetic success. If I

16

cannot successfully analyze *Evryali*, obviously I must first examine my own limitations. This does not embarass me since it's a particularly difficult score. But nevertheless, must something else be blamed? Isn't there an outburst of what we could temporarily call a xenakian style in this score which would be more than a soul-supplement? Xenakis speaks very little of style, though he arranged to compel computers to respect this notion which the profane can recognize only while listening. Xenakis barely touches upon the subject in his theoretical writings. Is this out of a sense of decency? Out of modesty? I don't know. Sometimes, an allusion, a short sentence will emerge concerning the beauty of this or that device, of this or that result, on the absurdity or the baseness of what Xenakis somewhere calls "the lowest strata of musical intelligence."

Iannis, you speak too little about this xenakian style. You can respond by saying that you leave that up to your historiographers. They thank you for your trust in them. They certainly thank you less for your silence! If you could help them just a little bit, they would be even more grateful.

Would it be going beyond the limits of this thesis, *Arts/ Sciences: Alloys* to credit techniques with only a secondary role, a role which serves only in relation to intuitions or aesthetic intentions which, most certainly, tend toward alloys or even end up becoming alloys? The techniques, however, do not subjugate themselves to the alloys. In short, what presides over all of that, what "inspires" (as they used to say) the totality of these approaches? Perhaps here we are venturing beyond the limits of your thesis. Nevertheless, it would be a bit paradoxical to have Xenakis right here, obliged to answer in some way because of the particular situation (laughs), and still not ask him what's going on or what is being protected behind this scientific fortress, behind this front of computers.

How is it that Xenakis convinces himself and us about this wonderful power of knowledge, a power which I myself believe in (up to a certain point), while in the meantime, he writes his most brilliant works simply with a pencil and paper? If you please, Iannis, where in this realm have things changed so totally and profoundly since Bach or Mozart, for example?

IANNIS XENAKIS

The last question is a very important one, in my mind. The answer is that I have sometimes been accused of being calculating, of being a mathematician, of being "dry," and all these in opposition to being a musician. This accusation is now out of date. Today it seems that I am no longer subject to it. Even musicians consider me a musician! This is a parenthesis I would like to open. For the first time, I find myself in an institution as "respectable" as the Université de Paris and even the Sorbonne. Up until now, I was always kind of "on the fringe," and little by little I'm putting this newly established position in order (since I now teach at Université de Paris*) by defending this thesis. It's true that almost all my writings refer to questions which can be demonstrated and expressed in a language which everyone understands, be it here, in Japan, in America, even by the Eskimos. On the other hand, the part which cannot be expressed, can be said only by art itself, by music itself or by the architecture or visual expressions themselves, and even then, I don't know if there are many things one can say, aside from "I like that" or "I don't like that" or "that's beautiful" or "that's ugly" or "that's revolting" or "that's fantastic," "interesting," etc. It's true that we fall back into aesthetic or psychological problems, but what can be said about construction or sonorities, etc., without using a technical or analogical or proportional or achitectural language? What can be said?

There is no language which could encompass these questions aside from the questions themselves which deal with construction, structures, rules and laws. But I agree with you: there is something else in music, in any music, even in the "ugliest" music. But, this "something" is neither distinguishable nor discernible; it is "unspeakable." It's the traits which are not yet describable. It is the art-object which must express them. That is why it's sort of an amputated aspect, no?

OLIVIER REVAULT D'ALLONNES

That's clever . . .

IANNIS XENAKIS

What do you mean, "clever"?

*Xenakis holds the position of lecturer at the Université de Paris I (Sorbonne) since 1973. (Translator's Note.)

OLIVIER REVAULT D'ALLONNES

You tell me that you can't answer, yet you yourself make comparisons between works of the past and a certain number of current trends.

IANNIS XENAKIS

I can do that! I can speak of structures. That's what I just said. But I can neither question nor speak of something's value when it is not immediately perceptible on a structural level. For example, you said that I calculate either with computers or "by hand," but amidst all that, there is still a style which comes through, independent of these calculations or any "metacalculation."

OLIVIER REVAULT D'ALLONES

Or "infracalculations," I don't know . . .

IANNIS XENAKIS

Or "infra." I would still say "meta," or "behind," which comes down to the same thing! I could even generalize here. I'll bet that any choice presupposes an arbitrary choice. There is no man-made construction which is not arbitrary in some way. To accept the laws which govern something's construction is already an arbitrary act. In mathematics we encounter this when modern as well as ancient mathematics arbitrarily sets axioms and then, only at a secondary stage, uses formalistic logic and thereby builds their entire structures. The group of axioms is set at the base or at the summit, in my mind, since the base is inversed. The point is on the ground and the base is in the sky since there is more room for it to grow there. That which is axiomatic infers an arbitrary choice. But is it completely arbitrary? Yes, but after first separating certain theoretical necessities added to the conditionings of actual and historical experience.

OLIVIER REVAULT D'ALLONNES

Nevertheless, there is a parallel which you yourself make. I believe it's in the latest edition of *Musique. Architecture.* and also at the end of your thesis report.* A parallel is drawn between the history of mathematical thinking and the history of musical forms, plus practically a third element, a third parallel which is not, of course,

---

*cf. Appendix I, p. 99

at all parallel, and which is the history of musical taste. Just as the fugue is a musical structure of the fugal period, so are your works typical of the twentieth century. But of course there is Xenakis the individual, and it seems to me that this totality is not arbitrary.

IANNIS XENAKIS

I'm afraid we are drifting a bit from the question you asked earlier since what you are talking about is a question of musicology and forms, or better yet, a science of forms and of historical revolutions. If the fugue was, in fact, fundamental at a given moment, it was certainly not so before its discovery, before it imposed itself! The fugue is by no means fundamental today. That's for sure! Therefore, this is first and foremost a technical problem, since what is, after all, a fugue? It's a group of rules and procedures with a view toward constructing a musical edifice. This group of rules was born. Consequently, it did not exist before that! And now it no longer exists in the broad sense, from the point of view of creative invention. This rather convincingly proves its at-least-partially arbitrary character.

OLIVIER REVAULT D'ALLONNES

The question was not about fugues but about your work, Iannis!

IANNIS XENAKIS

If I try to explain my ideas in books and articles or in lectures on this or that technique, it is because I can easily speak of these things. Or, when I teach, it's to incite others to delve into these same questions. But I don't say everything, even if I sense or perceive it, because I don't know how to say it. Therefore, eventually, I have the students listen and see the results. There you have a quick summary of my answer. Perhaps I didn't answer your other question . . .

OLIVIER REVAULT D'ALLONNES

Yes, perhaps . . . One is tempted to ask you: Why is there a certain historical gap between the arts and sciences and in what measure is there not more of a unilateral contribution directed from the sciences toward the arts rather than the opposite? That's one question; and the second one is: If this alloy-ing which you propose between the sciences and arts is something utopian (therefore

creative), doesn't that imply something other than a simple transformation in the realm of the arts and sciences? For instance, almost a transformation of civilization?

IANNIS XENAKIS

That's perfect, because I had noted more or less the same thing!
It brings one back to Olivier Revault D'Allonnes' first question,
which points out a delay . . . a one way street in the wrong direction . . . why have the roads narrowed with time?

I believe it's a question of civilization. Antiquity had also
witnessed this free movement between the arts and sciences. We
see Polycletes trying to apply geometry to sculpture with his
canon; this same free movement which similarly occurred in architecture, painting and music. Aristoxenus' text came later, as a
follow-up. I believe the fundamental point of the Renaissance
was its rediscovery of man's uniqueness. Man is something unique,
singular. There are not many men, there is but one. This man
encompasses all thinking and acting possibilities, and consequently, the interpretation between the sciences and arts. On the
other hand, the arts too have contributed to scientific thought in a
direct or indirect manner at certain crucial moments in history.

This is what I have tried to show in the table which I added to the
last chapter of *Musique. Architecture.* by drawing a parallel
especially between musical and mathematical thinking.* What is
indeed curious and immediately jumps off the page is that music is
much closer to mathematics than any of the other arts. Why? I'm
not going to show that now. However, I can say that the eye is
quicker, much more immediate and in direct contact with reality,
than the ear, which is less agile and more recessed, demanding
reflective thinking. Consequently, the ear must be more abstract
and therefore create bases which also are more abstract, bringing
them closer to mathematics. It is with this type of idea that I have
tried to show the tendril between music theory (and hence, a part
of music) and mathematical theory: how they coil around each
other, although they do, at times, go about in parallel motion
without coiling at all. Today, the artist's domain is behind the
times. I was already struck by the poverty of "combinatory"
thought in music before leaving the Athens Polytechnical School
where I studied compositional procedures. This is also true for
serial music which I later studied.

*op. cit. (Appendix I, p. 99)

21

Here, I would like to pay tribute to Olivier Messiaen. He was the only one whose thinking was completely open to these topics. Some of his work rested on the premise of "interventions." Furthermore, I believe that this came about thanks to the artistic side of his nature. But this is entirely another facet which does not belong to structural ones. Also, let's take another example: Olivier Messiaen's Modes of Limited Transposition. These were the beginning of my work on scales. Without generalizing, this beginning certainly allowed me to grasp some of the difficult principles of musicians' mental structures: their ways of thinking and acting.

Over fifteen years ago, I came upon these scale problems in musical composition. In the course of my work, I was led to resolve them with the help of almost-already-made mathematics. The result was my "Sieve theory."* It's not the opposite; I have almost never done the opposite. Compared to what mathematics offers the artist today, this is really nothing; it is minimal. What must be done then? Well, in my opinion, a concrete transformation of the musician's (the artist's as well as the scientist's) training. This training must not occur too late. It should start in grammar school, if not in nursery school. And it's all a problem of education, of the educational system, of man's training (from infancy to adolescence, and even later, up to his death); this is what is in question. Yet this separation between the literati (or artists) and the scientists occurs very early on, and it's a question of up-bringing, from the baby bottle onward. This results in a delay since there is no communication at all. In any case, the consequent lack of free movement and contact makes itself deeply felt. Moreover, this is why I have agreed to teach, to give lectures and seminars. Also, now at CEMAMu, we are making an effort to utilize the most advanced technology known to information theory in pedagogic directions. By combining problems of musical composition and thinking with those of space and vision and finally with those of mathematics (which the child necessarily learns when five, six, or seven years old), a revolutionary approach to music can be attempted. I think the core of the problem lies here. It's the question of man's survival, in harmonious surroundings, of course admitting contradictions, but affording richer surroundings than he knows at this time. Therefore, this differentiation is a residue of recent history. Little by little, the artist has strayed and has made

*cf. Appendix II, p. 103.

a sort of selection. He has examined only one of the aspects of art: precisely, the inexpressible aspect.

BERNARD TEYSSÈDRE

I believe that Michel Serres would like to intervene on certain points.

MICHEL SERRES

I would like to defend this thesis instead of Xenakis and for just one minute would like to answer Olivier Revault d'Allonnes. He poses the problem of exchanges between the sciences and arts. He would like to know if the exchange is not unbalanced; in other words, if you haven't borrowed some mathematical techniques while mathematics, on the other hand, hasn't taken anything from music. The reverse thesis would say that music is a step ahead, that Xenakis' music is in advance. I don't see the problem as being one of exchange (which would be a commercial point of view), nor from the point of view of scientific techniques. It's one thing to say that one borrows techniques from a given aspect of science and another thing to say that in his music, Xenakis presents a *general* idea of scientific thinking. The scientific world has changed and no one has become aware of this, perhaps not even the scientists.

What has changed is not that combinatory algebra has been replaced by group theory nor that Fourier transformations have been replaced by information theory. That is not important. What *is* important is that something called a "paradigm" has been completely transformed. A new world, a new scientific world has emerged in the second half of the twentieth century. The first to have stated this was not a philosopher, not a scientist, not an epistomologist, but Xenakis. It's Xenakis who first showed what a symbol detached from its background actually is; it's Xenakis who was the first to use not this or that mathematical technique, but only the most important and significant among them. To say that there is a delay has no meaning unless the problem is posed on local exchanges. If it is the global vision which is thrown into question, it can be found with Xenakis. All the traditional discourses hide this general vision of science and this paradigm from us. No, Xenakis, you are one step ahead and thank you for being there. (laughs and "bravos")

OLIVIER REVAULT D'ALLONNES

Michel Serres has just shown how the minds of numerous scholars can be opened by approaches such as Xenakis'. I never doubted that. My initial question was what could music (for example) bring not only to scholar-scientists, but to science itself. It's here that I see a certain gap and not a "delay"; moreover, we could define such a delay on the basis of which ideal calendar? Finally we are left with the problem of the social conditions of the "alloy" in question.

IANNIS XENAKIS

Fine, thank you very much; that answers the first question (laughs). I couldn't have said it better myself. The second question concerns this "social transformation." Naturally, it's a question . . . but I don't know which social transformation you mean in this case. This particular problem has remained absent from all the social transformations which are produced in the entire world. No one has answered this problem and I think I will come back to what I said earlier: the desired social transformation would be the one which would tackle the coexistence and interpenetration of these aspects of human life from the earliest education onward.

OLIVIER REVAULT D'ALLONNES

Speaking of pedagogy, it seems clear to me that neither innocently nor by chance, pedagogy, such as it is practiced in our society, creates literati on the one hand, and on the other hand, scientists, as you were saying.

IANNIS XENAKIS

Yes, it is certain that if one trains only scientists, it's probably due primarily to the time factor involved in specialization. But I believe that we can go beyond this stage. I myself have worked in at least two professions simultaneously, and I think that it's entirely possible to do even three and not only superficially, but by pushing these professions toward research. It's also a question of submission . . . I won't say of class struggle because it's much more nuanced and complex than that. But it goes without saying that it comes down to the question of a ramification of man's organization which produces spiritual and intellectual invalids. That's for sure. In my opinion these illnesses can be cured. How can we attain this radical pedagogical and also socio-environmental change? This is a reform which politics should be undertaking instead of

24

merely asking questions about salaries, technical stuff, improvements, social progress. The fulfillment of man's totality lies especially in this. I think that art (as well as science) has its role to play in putting everything together. What Michel Serres said is true: at the basis of art (and equally of science), there is this whole vision which can be called the vision of the twentieth century, which is a totality and which is hope, and finally which should be the hope of humanity.

BERNARD TEYSSÈDRE

Well, perhaps now we should give Olivier Messiaen the floor, since we have covered the first cycle of questions and answers.

Fig. 2. Cluny 2. Laser paths chosen for their excellent plastic qualities

DIALOGUE WITH
OLIVIER MESSIAEN

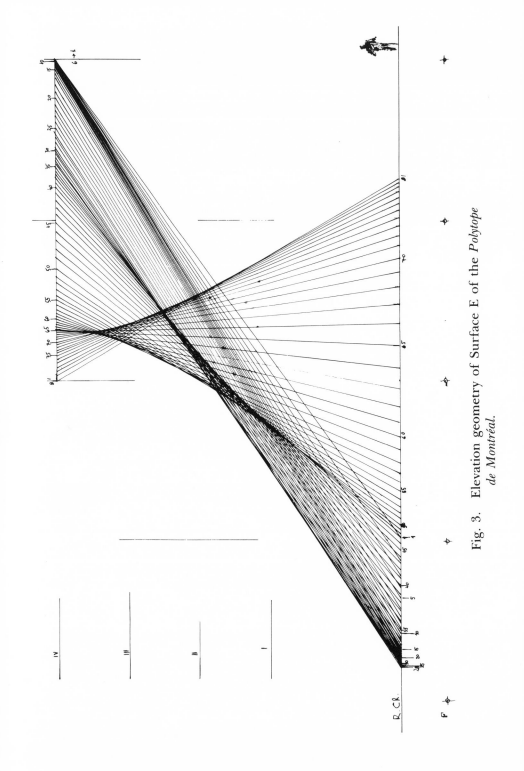

Fig. 3.   Elevation geometry of Surface E of the *Polytope de Montréal.*

OLIVIER MESSIAEN

A hero cannot be criticized! Therefore, I will ask only a few questions. But, dear friend, I wouldn't want these questions to seem to be indiscreet to you. If they displease you, say so. These are not really questions, but more like requests for elucidations to enable you to clarify your thoughts. Instead of making a brilliant statement like my colleagues, I will simply ask you my questions one after the other. This will be easier for you, for me, for everyone.

First question: somewhere in your thesis and also at several places in your book *Musique. Architecture.*, you seem to lead history, and especially the beginnings of music, back to the birth of scales and modes, and scale-constructs. Before these scales (and you yourself recognize this) only tetrachords were utilized. But, don't you think there was first of all the "cry" at the very beginning of humanity? Shouts of joy and shrieks of pain: this is *exclamatory language* (spoken as well as musical). Then, the perception and imitation of other sounds, of the wind, of water, bird songs, etc.: this is *imitative language* (which is mostly music yet it can also be found in primitive onomatopeias). Syntactical spoken languages came much later as did organized musical phrases, and with these, preliminary, "outside-time" (as you call it) scales, modes, and scale-constructs. Why have you stopped at this scale material, to the exclusion of all the rest?

IANNIS XENAKIS

No, not at all. Would you like me to speak of this right away? It is true that I did not go any further, perhaps out of ignorance. I don't know what went on on the mind of the paleontological man, a million or two million or even thirty million years ago, as we have just discovered. We have no way of knowing the form of his thinking. If I look upon past centuries from this present century, it is because I belong to this century and consequently can only speak of things which are comprehensible to me. I admit that it's doubtlessly a drawback not to be able to deal in greater depth with the questions you have raised.

Furthermore, what does it mean "to imitate"; what does it mean "to exclaim," which came before syntax, before all rules, before constructions, no matter how small they may be? This is already an indication of a recognition of form, therefore of a structural vision of the environment, admitting that man was sort of an object-unto-himself. Nature and his environment were something outside of him and what he perceived through his senses was consequently imitated. Here also I think it probably can be said that his being capable of imitating the sound of the wind, hail or thunder, etc., was a way of constructing, a primitive way perhaps, but nevertheless already very complex. Science today (and when I say science, I mean scientific thinking), has merely glimpsed over certain mental structures of man for only a very little time. Others will come, but it's difficult to speak of those; I can only speak of things which are already well formulated and visible. This is why I started with tetrachords, which are already at a rather advanced stage of construction. I must also add that tetrachords are part of a cultural, scientific or organizational approach, meaning a material. All the same, in other civilizations such as those of Japan or China or Africa, all very ancient, even more ancient than Greek civilization (we don't know too much about the Egyptian), there are other approaches where the tetrachord doesn't play a role. For example: in Nô music, there is the interval of a fourth. We could say that the fourth is a sort of universal reality, but the interior construction of the fourth is something perhaps specific to the third or fourth century before the Christian era in the Greek world. Since tetrachords were at the base of the diatonic system, and hence of all music up until our present epoch, they can be viewed as the historical and musicological guiding line which enables us to extrapolate further. This is not so true for earlier periods (which I call pre-logical, even though they are not at all pre-logical in the musical realm). And what you tell us is fundamental because even if we want to dig more deeply into these questions of structures today, it would be necessary to come back to, or, more precisely, distance ourselves from these same structures, from these musical concepts, which, besides, would now tend toward extra-musical reasoning.

Now, let's look at these things with a completely new eye or ear, with new tools. This is the recognition of forms. If we received (and in fact, we do receive) signals from intrastellar, galactic space, well, it would be necessary to know how to distinguish these from noise (as Michel Serres said earlier), to see if they are structured, if they are coherent, and if this coherency is meaningful or not. By meaningful, I mean to say if it comes from natural sources (which is to say, from nature itself) or if it comes from other beings who would resemble man. It would be necessary to go back, well before all structures, before all forms of thought which we have received from civilization and schooling, and to get back to pre-rational, pre-logical, pre-structural, pre-syntactical situations. I don't know if I have answered your question.

OLIVIER MESSIAEN

That's a very beautiful response. But you have also said that the past was in the future and the future in the past. This is why I allowed myself to touch upon some regions where our knowledge becomes feeble.

Second question, absolutely personal: You know as well as I do that a certain number of objects gives a certain number of permutations, and the more the number of objects increases, the more the number of permutations increases and with a speed and in quantitites which can seem disproportioned. So, three objects give six permutations, six objects give seven hundred and twenty, and twelve objects give (if I'm not mistaken) four hundred ninety seven million, one thousand six hundred permutations. Suppose these objects correspond to durations: I would have to write out these durations in order to know what gesture or what movement they could create in time. There has been a lot of talk about retrograde movement these days: this is but one movement, one single movement among thousands of others, and its permutation follows the original trajectory. And all the other permutations? I can't write out the millions and millions of permutations . . . and yet I must write them out in order to know them and to love them (I insist on the verb *to love*!). In your case, a machine will give you the millions of permutations within a few minutes: it's a cold and unexplicit list. How can and do you choose directly from within this immense world of possibilities without intimate knowledge or love?

IANNIS XENAKIS

I believe there are two questions grouped together in your last question. The first is the question of love; fine. The second is the possible choice among a large quantity of possibilities . . .

OLIVIER MESSIAEN

And I believe you are going to answer M. d'Allonnes' first question . . .

IANNIS XENAKIS

Perhaps, I don't know. The question then of having to love something in order to use it naturally implies an initial taming. To tame or "win over" means live with, and live with means to love and also to not love; for loving leads to its corollary.

OLIVIER MESSIAEN

I've expressed myself poorly. What I wanted to say was "to know!" To know with a real and emotional knowledge, out of love or hate . . .

IANNIS XENAKIS

Yes, that's the emotional side, the epiphenomenon of knowledge,; the pain, or on the contrary, the joy, or the two together which one can experience when loving a beautiful woman, for example. But possessing something out of love or hate is perhaps one form and consequently, the only possible form, of knowledge.

When I look at the starry sky, I love it in a certain way because I know it in a certain way; but if I must know the successive stages of astrophysics, well, that may happen without love. Love would here be surpassed by a kind of revelation which is beyond this epiphenomenon called love. Consequently, I can handle the concepts of things themselves without being in direct possession of them, under the condition that I may conceive of them and feel them from within in some way. This is the beginning of an answer to your question, which I find to be fundamental. All this means is that even if I am incapable of dominating a certain phenomenon, I am capable of obtaining a truth which is inherent to the conceived or observed phenomenon, thanks to a kind of immediate revelation. Henceforth, I can accept and use this, in and as itself. When I tape record a sound which I find interestting, I don't know exactly what is in this sound. I perceive things which interest me and I use them. Therefore, I cannot love the things within this sound which are so refined that I cannot totally perceive them. I am not consciously nor unconsciously capable of naming them, but I accept the whole, in itself, since I am attracted by that.

OLIVIER MESSIAEN

You are attracted, therefore there is a revelation!

IANNIS XENAKIS

That's right, yes.

OLIVIER MESSIAEN

A revelation is like falling in love, like a thunderbolt. It's the Romantics' *inspiration.*

IANNIS XENAKIS

Yes, I don't deny that at all. On the contrary.

OLIVIER REVAULT D'ALLONNES

I didn't know you were a romantic, Iannis! (Laughs)

IANNIS XENAKIS

I said earlier, (or maybe I didn't) that in the artistic realm there is revelation. In philosophy, in knowledge, it's the same thing. Yes, revelation is absolutely indispensable. It's one of man's crutches. He has two crutches: revelation and inference. And in the artistic realm, both are valid. In the scientific domain, there is one which takes precedence over the other, and that is inference.

To get to the second part of your question, that is, how does one choose from a great wealth of possibilities? Well, there are many ways of going about it. I can imagine—I don't need a machine for that—I can imagine and intellectually make a choice. There are several ways of making this choice. It's true that when there are a few sounds, or more precisely, a few pitches to control, it is easy to proceed in an arbitrary or intuitive manner, directly. But, when it's a question of a great quantity of sounds, well, there it would be handy to borrow from other domains. When I look at a small number of individuals, I see them as individuals; I see their relationships, their characteristics, and their relations to space and time, their own physiognomies, etc. But if there is a crowd, I can no longer distinguish the individuals, because they are too numerous. On the contrary, what I can see are the aspects, the characteristics of the crowd. When I need a great number of possibilities, I must manage to use characteristics of large numbers; which are, for example, density traits, traits of order or disorder, spacial distribution, sound-space distribution (such as pitch, time, order, disorder, etc. dimensions), and there we find potential tools to make certain choices. I am not saying that this applies to all choices, but we can thus eliminate a fair number from this apparent impossibility of choice within such a vast number of elements. I am going under the principle that man is incapable of saying "yes, I mean this object which is there," when the density is too great. A certain hesitation while choosing is permissible at such times because other characteristics are then important. It's the same phenomenon which was produced when probabilistic calculations were introduced into the kinetic theory of gases. In any case, it was a little different in that it was a problem of calculation and not a psychological problem. We arrived at the kinetic theory of gases, that is to say, concepts which enabled many different sciences, and not only thermodynamics, to make great leaps forward. I believe that in the artistic, sensory and also sensual realms, this is what's happening. Have I answered your question? Am I making any sense?

OLIVIER MESSIAEN

Yes, yes. Third question (this one is absolutely indiscreet and if you don't want to answer, you may do as you see fit!). In *Musique. Architecture.*, you quote a magnificent text of Parmenides which is generally applied to the universe and which contains the notion, among others, of "Being," or the quality of that which is.*
In summarizing this text to the optimum, these few words can be isolated: "it *is*," "without birth," "indestructible," "imperturbable," "without end," "being simultaneously one, continuous." Having studied theology, I can apply this only to God, since only divine attributes are expressed. Yet, you explain this text in terms of energy and energy conservation. I'm well aware that one of the new theories explaining the beginning of the universe is the explosion theory, which affirms that the universe started by a fantastic combustion. This presupposes an energetic force which itself could be considered a divine attribute. But I think your ex-

*cf., also *Formalized Music*, p. 202. (trans. note)

planation of Parmenides is altogether different. Can you tell us why you have chosen energy?

IANNIS XENAKIS

Parmenides' "Being" is one of the first texts where he tries to encompass what is "real." In order to accomplish this, he is obliged to detach himself from it, or make a sort of abstract definition of it, even if it is in contradiction with daily experience. This is what enabled Aristotle to say that Parmenides was crazy. It's true that what Parmenides says about "Being" corresponds to what could be said (as you yourself have indeed said) about a unique god. But on the other hand, if we don't think of theology or of any religion, but stay in the realm which is, I believe, simultaneously fundamental and much more universal (that of Parmenides), the text in no way indicates any reference to any god. He simply says that it's "the notion of Being." He speaks only of being, of being as existence, not an active being. This is why he doesn't put the notion of being in the infinitive. As contradictory as Parmenides' direction may seem in relation to reality, I think it is one of the revelatory sparks among the conflicts of human thinking, all while trying to envelop man's problems throughout the ages.

Now, there is but one spectral answer to Parmenides' notion of "Being" and that is this correlation I made between it and energy because I found this to be the closest in content (in the scientific domain) to what he describes. Because energy is, in fact, something which fills the world. The principle of energy conservation is, of course, just one principle, but one which holds fast to this definition of "Being." Therefore, I have tried to give an answer in nature's realm, meaning science and physics. By no means is this an exclusive answer; it's merely a sort of comparison that I make. I don't say that "Being" is this, but it does strangely call up the definition or, more precisely, the conception of energy which fills the world. Energy has no known beginning nor end since, due to the principle of energy conservation, there could be no end nor beginning. This, of course, is a bit in contradiction with the theory concerning the explosion of the original atom, at the outset of our extremely condensed universe. But I am allowed to think of this as a temporary theory, as are all theories. This comparison of Parmenides' "Being" with energy is only a kind of analogy. In fact, God's attributes are identical with those of "Being" since, subadjacently, man's same logic can be found.

OLIVIER MESSIAEN

Now, the fourth question . . .

IANNIS XENAKIS

If you please, to finish with Parmenides, I would like to mention one other fundamental thing which can be found in one of his fragments: It's the question of the equivalence between a being and thinking, which is also one of the guiding lines in man's thought throughout the ages. In one verse which has remained famous, and which Plato reproduced in his *Republic*, Parmenides said, "For it is the same to be and to think." Yet, the structure of the sentence is symmetrical in relation to the verb "is." To be, meaning "Being" and thought are the same thing. This is where I see the symmetry. Much later on, there is dissymmetry when Descartes states "I think, therefore I am." It's curious to note when comparing these two sentences (which, I do believe, is necessary) that it demonstrates precisely the same preoccupation throughout the ages. I don't know whether Descartes knew . . .

BERNARD TEYSSÈDRE

It's not at all the same.

IANNIS XENAKIS

No, "I think, therefore I am" is asymmetrical and if we look to the solipsists, to Berkeley, for example, there we have another inversion which is reminiscent of Descartes', but which leads to another direction. This means that objective reality, or "Being," cannot at all "be" except as thought. This is to say that there is an identification between "Being" and thought, outside of any reality. If Descartes is a realist, Berkeley suddenly becomes abstract with his solipsism, and everything comes back to "thought." Since then, of course, there has been nineteenth century philosophy with marxist reasoning which admitted an objectivity that is independent from man and there has also been science which is ambiguous because of the memorable failures of its succesive theories of classical mechanics, etc. And we haven't seen the end of it! This is why scientists say today, "Everything happens as if . . ."

OLIVIER MESSIAEN

Fourth and last question: from page eight on of the French translation of the last chapter of your book *Formalized Music* which you have included among the documents submitted as your thesis file, you give several methods of microcomposition based on probability distribution.* Under Method 4, I found the following sentence: "The random variable moves between two reflecting elastic barriers." It's very poetic and thanks to it, I can wallow in an abyss of daydreaming . . . Later, you give the calculated explanation, which I did not understand. Could you give us another explanation of this process with a concrete musical example, perhaps from one of your works?

IANNIS XENAKIS

Method 4 refers to the basic hypothesis which can be found in the previous pages, starting on page 242,** "New Proposal in Microcomposition Based on Probability Distributions." This refers to pressure-time space, the pressure which your eardrum receives from atmospheric air in the course of time. So if we consider that this pressure takes on greater or lesser values, expressable in numbers, we can make pressure correspond to notes placed on a pitch axis and then we could write this on a music staff. We will obtain a passageway, a variety of pitches in function of time, forming a continuous melodic curve.

In the case of pressure-time periodic space (where a square, triangular, or sine wave can be formed) the sound wave repeats itself identically and systematically. But if the variation is not periodic, it will adopt curves possessing just about any sinuosity. We could imagine that this curve is drawn by a floating point moving on a plane, without ever retracing its steps, neither in pitch-time space nor in pressure-time space, which comes down to the same thing from the point of view of its path's definition.

These paths will obviously depend on the laws which will set the moving point in motion. Periodic functions are very strict laws which correspond to melodies or equally to boring sounds. Probability theories and their mathematical combinations can, on the contrary, produce very free paths which never repeat themselves and which correspond to much richer melodies and sounds. The only thing is, these probabilistic treks can take on any value.

*cf. Appendix II , p. 112 of present volume.
**cf. Appendix III, p. 109 of present volume.

Consequently, they can make the moving point surpass the weakest limits of the ear. In other words, in the case of pressure-time space, there could be pressures equal to those of the atomic bomb! Therefore it is necessary to limit untimely growth, these colossal probabilistic energies! It's exactly the same case with a bullet which is channelled by a gun barrel while it ricochets off the barrel's inner walls.

OLIVIER MESSIAEN

It's what you call barriers . . .

IANNIS XENAKIS

They are elastic barriers . . .

OLIVIER MESSIAEN

They reflect . . .

IANNIS XENAKIS

Because they reflect inwardly, following the law of elastic planes' reflection, without loss, without absorbing energy. In other words, the pathway created by a probabilitistic or stochastic process is reflected as if it were off a mirror when it reaches the chosen barriers. It is, if you please, exactly like intervallic inversions. In melodic inversion, the intervals are reflected in a horizontal mirror placed in retrograde on the time axis. It's a reflection in a vertical mirror. These are the very same and simple principles which can be found all over, even in music. At present, we can imagine nonreflecting surfaces with fields of gravitation; finally, all kinds of forces (in the abstract sense of the term, of course.)

OLIVIER MESSIAEN

This is absolutely wonderful . . . So, as far as I'm concerned, I have finished. But earlier, when Olivier Revault d'Allonnes spoke, I didn't intervene. He was making such a brilliant speech—I didn't dare interrupt! Perhaps he would now like to bring up some of his purely musical questions, seeing that I have the good fortune to have the floor?

OLIVIER REVAULT D'ALLONNES

Personally, I failed. He, Xenakis, didn't speak!

OLIVIER MESSIAEN

It's not out of malice, but out of curiousity, instinctive appeal, and also out of admiration . . .

OLIVIER REVAULT D'ALLONNES

I wanted Xenakis to speak of his compositional style, and he gave me simultaneously a most satisfying yet very hermetic answer. He told me, "Listen, I have nothing to add. Listen, and if you don't understand, listen again. And then, like it, if you like it."

OLIVIER MESSIAEN

There's a certain modesty in that which surprises me personally because I'm not in the same profession as he is. I teach composition class at the Conservatoire*where, for the past forty years, I've spent my time decortiting musical works, trying to figure out what happens in them . . . These things of which you don't dare speak, which scare you, I deal with all day long . . .

IANNIS XENAKIS

It's true, I remember very well. I was in your musical analysis class, and what interested me the most was precisely the lectures you held on the subject of technique. . . (laughs) because all the rest amounted to, "As we were saying, that's beautiful, isn't it?"

OLIVIER MESSIAEN

I didn't really say it very much. I kept quiet!

IANNIS XENAKIS

This is true; it was rare, but you did say this sometimes. But that's all you said about the problem of style. Or perhaps style no longer is a question of technique, so then it must be something else. For me, style refers to technique as well as to music's "perfumes" (which may just be more interesting), and on several levels besides.

OLIVIER MESSIAEN

Yes, but aside from all structures, it seems to me that each individual and every particular musician (since we're speaking of music) possesses what we call in philosophy "his accidents," his

*Conservatoire National Superieur de Musique de Paris; Messiaen taught harmony, analysis, and composition there from 1942 to 1978. (Translator's note.)

"tics," his personal habits. A second or third Xenakis who would try to write Xenakis' music in your place, using the same structures, would certainly not obtain the same results. There is, then, a question of personal style.

IANNIS XENAKIS

Yes, I'll admit that . . .

OLIVIER MESSIAEN

One immediately recognizes Xenakis' music. Not only because of the glissandi or permutations; one can recognize it because of a certain sonority, a certain way of orchestrating, a certain way of distributing the sounds which differs from all others.

IANNIS XENAKIS

Perhaps the answer to Olivier Revault d'Allonnes' question is the following: In life, there are two ways of proceeding: one is to do things and the other is to analyze them. But the best analysis, for me, is to do things; in other words, I refuse analysis—psychoanalysis, if you prefer—as a method of introspection. If one gets involved in these domains, one doesn't know what is going to be discovered, and one risks falling into holes, dreadful traps. Therefore it's a tactic, and that's why I insist on saying that it's the "thing," music itself, which is not hermetic as opposed to an analytical discourse which is hermetic.

OLIVIER MESSIAEN

And nevertheless, I question the sphinx every day, since I have an analysis class, and I'm not at all unhappy. That doesn't prevent me from making music!

IANNIS XENAKIS

Outside of technical questions, don't you give other answers?

OLIVIER MESSIAEN

I handle only technical questions.

IANNIS XENAKIS

So . . .

OLIVIER MESSIAEN

Outside of purely musical fact, of course, I would not allow myself to reconcile intentions because I would certainly be incapable of doing so. Or if I do it, it's only very occasionally.

IANNIS XENAKIS

But what do you mean when you say musical technique? Isn't it, in fact, a question of proportions, durations, combinations?

OLIVIER MESSIAEN

I do often speak of durations, harmonies, modes, colors. I know that you don't believe in this . . .

IANNIS XENAKIS

In my opinion, it's already outside the realm of technique.

OLIVIER MESSIAEN

Orchestration is also a question of technique in my opinion.

IANNIS XENAKIS

Which means one can speak of these things.

OLIVIER MESSAEN

It is technical: perfectly, purely and completely musical. It's on this point, it seems to me, that Olivier Revault d'Allonnes tried to question you.

OLIVIER REVAULT D'ALLONNES

. . . As well as what is next to and underlying technique. I don't believe I'm revealing any secret in saying that one day I saw Xenakis at his work table. He was working on a piece. Reviewing it, he was stopped by a detail. He said: "Oh no, that's going to be horrible," and he changed it. So that then is technique? (laughs) I believe that happens to all composers.

MICHEL SERRES

In a word, we're getting back to the question of choice.

IANNIS XENAKIS

Yes, of arbitrary, intuitive, etc., choice.

MICHEL SERRES

... That which can be called inspiration, if you wish, but which remains a choice.

OLIVIER REVAULT D'ALLONNES

So there we avoid diving into the muddy regions of subjectivity?

IANNIS XENAKIS

Isn't the best way to dive into it precisely by making music?

OLIVIER REVAULT D'ALLONNES

To choose among a vast number of possibilities seemed to be a difficult problem for Olivier Messiaen. Actually, any sensory organ, the ear, the eye, even touch, functions in exactly the same manner, receiving an enormous quantity of information in such a way that you must contrast the constitutive elements (which thereby establishes the technical problem of choice making); to choose among the millions of possibilities in front of you, on the one hand, and on the other, the subjective problem of saying (as they say "off the cuff") "that's dreadful." It's exactly the same thing. The "cuff," or the ear or the eye, functions in exactly the same manner as a computer, meaning it receives fifty million bits of information that it sorts out and faithfully transmits. Consequently, there is no opposition between what you call power, inspiration, event, "sensorality" and on the other hand, this problem which you find so difficult; that is to say, making a choice among a vast number of elements. That's how it works, in living flesh.

IANNIS XENAKIS

In set theory, there is even Zermelo's famous axiom regarding choice, which postulates that we can choose an element in a given set either in an arbitrary manner or with the help of "revelation." This is mathematical and the mathematics used here are wholly aesthetic, I dare say. Here is the problem, and calculating machines are the filters.

OLIVIER MESSIAEN

Simulators.

IANNIS XENAKIS

Choice simulators, housing the rules which enable choice making. Man, with his ear and senses, makes much more complex choices than a computer can today. In other words, choice simulation is still very rudimentary compared to man's capabilities.

OLIVIER REVAULT D'ALLONNES

Yes, we still don't know how to command the computer. Sensory terminals do it without knowing how they do it.

OLIVIER MESSIAEN

I'll give you a concrete example. When I note bird songs, I do it with paper and pencil. Sometimes my wife accompanies me and tape records these same songs which I'm copying down. Yet, when we sit home and listen to what the recorder has captured, I can't help but notice how unmerciful the machine has been. It recorded everything, including horrible noises which have no relation to what I went to find. I hadn't heard these noises: I heard only the bird. Why didn't I hear these other noises? That's it, there's a "Why?" Because my ears, of course, acted as filters.

IANNIS XENAKIS

This is what can be called intelligent or directional hearing. It corresponds to one of the choice criteria you unknowingly imposed upon yourself because you wanted to hear only bird songs amidst all the forest sounds.

OLIVIER MESSIAEN

My attention was directed to the birds, and I heard them, but I heard them at the exclusion of disagreeable sounds such as passing cars or planes. . .

IANNIS XENAKIS

At the exclusion of other sounds. Moreover, in information theory, anything which is not the desired or a selected signal is dismissed as being noise.

OLIVIER MESSIAEN

We hear what we want to hear.

MICHEL SERRES

We hear signals.

IANNIS XENAKIS

Yes. And the difficulty in appreciating any work is in choosing precisely what is important. That's why when you hear a piece of Bach which has already been played a hundred, a thousand times, it can seem altogether different than what you're used to hearing, depending on the choices you make at that given moment. It's not only a given work-in-itself which is interesting, but also the individual and personal choice of the listener. That's why Newton, suddenly getting hit on the nose by the falling apple, said, "I've found it!"

OLIVIER REVAULT D'ALLONNES

All of this tells us more or less how you Iannis, conceive of choice, but not how you decide what is "dreadful" or the contrary. And who can we ask if not you, the composers?

OLIVIER MESSIAEN

Bach fugues were mentioned earlier, when we spoke of structures. Yet there is nothing more structural and (excuse me) more boring than an academic fugue. Bach wrote thousands of fugues; they're all over, in all of his works, in his cantatas, Passions, his mass, organ works, and in his keyboard works. These fugues are never structured like academic fugues, and they are different from all other fugues written during the same period, because they possess a certain melodic joy and harmonic control which belong only to "Papa" Bach.

IANNIS XENAKIS

Yes, I believe the problem is there.

OLIVIER MESSIAEN

I'll take it even further. In Bach one finds a little of what you have. Sometimes, there are superimposed intentions! For example, in certain chorals there is the the choral line which Bach didn't alter because it was a sacred text. He left it as such. It was willed, *intentional*. In the lowest bass part, there is an ostinato which is also *intentional*. In the inner voices, there is chromaticism: this too is *intentional* and he doesn't let up. The three superimposed intentions account for the extraordinary encounters, modern chords and counterpoints, which could almost be signed by Debussy. There is, perhaps, one way of understanding how structure can give birth to something new and personal.

IANNIS XENAKIS

In a more contemporary light, a fugue structure is not totalitary, meaning it reveals free and less-clearly defined parts, and schema which are more or less followed. But with these schema, there are "data entries," (as these are called in information theory today) which allow you to obtain different results from these same schema. Large quantities of intelligence (in the broadest sense) and contradictory intentions can be included in these data entries, which are free in themselves. But these schema can be translated by a kind of system or automaton since they function autonomously, and the fugue's significant lead over all the scientific thinking of its time occurred precisely because the fugue proposed systems which science then ignored. Only for a short time has science been systematically preoccupied with its own systematic methods; in other words, stochastic or determinist clockworks.

MICHEL SERRES

No. In the seventeenth century, a little before Bach wrote fugues or before schools required fugal writing, all scientific thought occurred automatically. Finally, it's a demonstration of contemporaneity between the sciences and arts.

IANNIS XENAKIS

Yes, you're right. Descartes treats this extensively.

MICHEL SERRES

That's right, Descartes . . . Olivier de Serres.

IANNIS XENAKIS

But the abstract automaton was proposed only by musicians.

MICHEL SERRES

Ah, right, yes . . . that's possible . . . music boxes were the rage.

IANNIS XENAKIS

Musicians materialized the products proposed by the abstract automaton by playing them.

MICHEL SERRES

Yes, it's true, they were ahead of science, as usual.

BERNARD TEYSSÈDRE

But to get back to our topic . . . curiously, what is interesting in fugues is not the abstract automaton, in my opinion, but the specifically freer parts where Bach was able to introduce his personal genius.

IANNIS XENAKIS

Yes, but neither can we ignore the fact that here, in relation to other musical forms, we have an extremely compact form with a subadjacent structure onto which we can add other "forms." Naturally, the results would not have been the same if there had not been these subajacent structures, this schema.

BERNARD TEYSSÈDRE

Good enough. Seeing that the debate with Olivier Messiaen has dealt essentially with music, I believe the discussion with Michel Ragon will deal more particularly with architectural problems.

DIALOGUE WITH
MICHEL RAGON

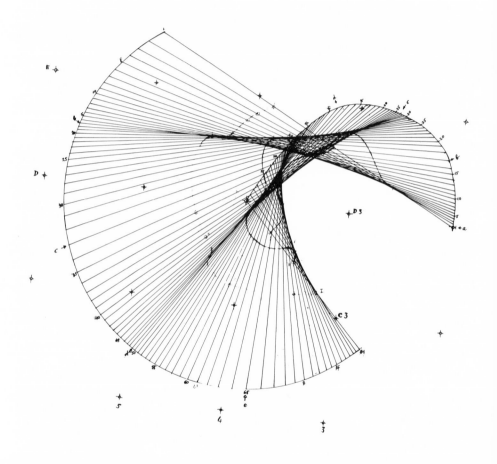

Fig. 4. Plan geometry of Surface E of the *Polytope de Montréal*.

MICHEL RAGON

In the course of this debate Xenakis' book *Musique. Architecture.* has been frequently quoted. It's one of the two books compiling all of Xenakis' texts, the other being *Formalized Music.* If this book is entitled *Musique. Architecture.*, it is precisely because two creative products are closely linked in Xenakis' work: music and architecture. If these two subjects were separated by Xenakis for a certain period, they are now absolutely reunited. They were separated at a time when we didn't really know Xenakis; that is to say, during the period when Xenakis was a "pure" (so to speak) architect, as Le Corbusier's collaborator. Xenakis worked for Le Corbusier for twelve years, I believe. You know that when one works for an architect, for a boss, all that one does, all that one produces under this boss, is obviously attributed to the boss. This is why I would like to draw attention to the two projects signed by Le Corbusier but which Xenakis worked on particularly. I mean the façade of the Tourette Convent in 1954, and it is easy enough to see that Xenakis worked on it since the architecture is conceived somewhat like a score. Then there is the Philips Pavilion in 1956, which one could call a "musical recepticle." These two works, conceived with Xenakis' participation in Le Corbusier's studio, have since been verified by Le Corbusier himself as being Xenakis' work. There are two texts by Le Corbusier at our disposal, quoted in *Musique. Archtecture,** which indicate Xenakis' considerable contribution to these works. I mention this in

---

Musique. Architecture.; pp. 151-152.

passing because certain architects deny Xenakis the right to appropriate works signed by Le Corbusier. Being less royalist than his students or disciples, Le Corbusier has in effect verified the works in question as being Xenakis'.

And then there are the *Polytopes*! Olivier Revault d'Allonnes has written a very copious book on the *Polytopes* which speaks of them better that I could even mention. In these transparent architectures of steel strings (which serve as a support to luminous points where light itself is architecture), light "architectures" space in ephemeral designs. This is also an important part of Xenakis' architectural work, and in this case, an architect's work intimately combined with that of a musician. There is also Xenakis' recurring utopia of a total *spectacle*. Without a doubt it's a total *spectacle* such as one could witness on that fabulous night at Persopolis* with the two hundred and fifty torch carriers which are so often alluded to. But also, it could encompass Xenakis' more recent ideas of casting out shining spiderweb-like canvases over cities and countrysides, to link the earth and the moon by luminous filaments, to create artificial aurora boreales ... all things of which he speaks, and about which you, Iannis Xenakis, tell us in your resumé accompanying your thesis file. Finally, there is another aspect of your work which I believe is better known, and that's why I would like to look into it. I'm referring to your prospective architectural project, or your utopian architecture. Let's go back to your chapter entitled "La Ville Cosmique" in *Musique. Architecture.*† I would like to ask you a few questions on this topic, since that is the rule of the game.

I will quote some passages from your text, "The Cosmic City." You begin by asking yourself if it isn't necessary to opt for an architectural decentralization and a decentralization of cities, or if, on the other hand, centralization should not be accepted. And you categorically favor the option of a centralization which no one could consider abusive. In other words, you object to the theory of linear cities (Le Corbusier is one of this theory's authors), which you accuse of being naïve. You propose to construct vertical, narrow cities which would reach up to three thousand, indeed even five thousand meters in altitude; therefore, cities not very vast, but entirely in metal: some kind of giant skyscrapers but

---

Persepolis, 1971, 8- or 4-track electroacoustic pieces, 57 minutes, including live light action. This work was premiered on the Persepolis mountain in Greece, among the ancient ruins of that site (trans. note)

† cf. p. 153, *Musique. Architecture.*

ones containing a city's complete morphology. You find that concentration is a vital necessity for humanity, as you say, and that it's necessary to completely change present urbanist and architectural ideas and replace them by others. This will therefore be my first question, even though this text is quite old. It dates from 1964. It's possible that you have evolved since then. Today's session is a chance to chat a little with you and ask you questions. I'm finally allowed to ask some questions I've wanted to ask you for a long time now. Do you still believe in this rather elaborate idea of centralization now, twelve years later? Do you think that it's necessary at a time when electronic energy dispersion, or natural energies such as solar or eolian energy can admit a decentralization which precisely has nothing in common with past decentralizations? In other words, where culture itself can easily be decentralized by electronic means? Do you believe that such an elaborate centralization is still necessary? Or has this idea become dated since you thought of it in 1964?

IANNIS XENAKIS

I believe that centralization (which I prefer to call a "densification") of human dwellings and relations is, first of all, a historical necessity which we can find in all examples of urban construction and human dwellings as well as in human relations, in culture, all over. What makes it even more necessary today is the pellicular invasion of planetary space by dispersed cities which destroys the environment. Actually, there are two tendencies: one of densification-toward-compaction (a greater densification); and the other is a centrifugal tendency which prefers to reintroduce rural habits in the middle of green nature, where possible. If this is not possible, then they must be created by artificial means. Each of these two tendencies is as natural as the other, but the compaction tendency becomes a necessity during industrial eras because of an inherently more explosive densification of human population. The second tendency is natural, because it corresponds to past nostalgias and also because our present cities are far from offering the natural environment which the human body and spirit demand. Actually, these two tendencies struggle against one another. In fact, the saturation (or compaction) tendency is winning out because of economic as well as all sorts of other reasons.

I still agree with what I proposed in 1964. I'm persuaded that it's a solution, perhaps a temporary one, but one which is more interesting and less criminal than dispersion over the global surface. Such a great densification does not mean that I refuse man's solitude, his right to isolate himself as an individual in this enormous beehive which is today's city. I say only that instead of spreading out over a surface, which creates problems of contact for human activities, we must organize cities in a vertical manner; This is not at all a new idea, since it already existed on a smaller scale in the argument which started in the twenties, when there was a question of having to choose between "garden cities" (as they were then called) and "vertical cities." Le Corbusier was one of the defenders of these vertical cities. But these vertical cities then corresponded only to the pure and simple dwelling, and not to an entire city. They didn't encompass all of a city's activities whereas I think that we must extend this principle to all of a city's activities for technical reasons, for reasons linked to human relations, and also in order to explore in greater depth what is left for us on this earth, and finally because such a system would allow us to install cities in truly uninhabitable climates, either very hot or cold climates and in overpopulated or deserted areas. I believe I've answered your first question.

MICHEL RAGON

This text was written twelve years ago. It is contemporary with other texts, other neighboring theories, for example, the "spatial city" of Yona Friedman, of Nicolas Schoffer's "cybernetic city," or even Paul Matmond's inhabited pyramids. How do you situate yourself in relation to these prospective architectural theories which were born at the same time as your theory?

IANNIS XENAKIS

I find them shy in comparison to mine! In reality, they are merely extrapolations on a relatively weak scale of what should be a very great concentration and, generally speaking, they refer only to individual dwellings and not to a city as a global phenomenon.

MICHEL RAGON

No one before our time had even envisioned a three or four or five-kilometer-high construction. The most utopian in this progression toward a vertical city, until you, was Frank Lloyd Wright and his project for a 1660-meter-high tower.

IANNIS XENAKIS

Yes, but this 1660-meter tower was an office building which had two faults: one, it wasn't high enough; and then, it was subordinate to its surface structure (which was constructed of "porticos") which, in the end, transformed this thing into a sort of 1660-meter-high obelisk.

MICHEL RAGON

This is true, it was a sort of obelisk, while you have invented some extremely interesting forms in your project.

IANNIS XENAKIS

That is to say it all happened out of a kind of revelation I had while designing the Philips pavilion, which is formed by S-curve surfaces; Because of some experiments which were done in a laboratory near Eindhoven in Holland, I realized that the S-curve was excessively resistant and its form could not be destroyed. These experiments were done because calculations based on the materials' resistance as well as on the theory of elasticity did not at all allow foreseeing it through to the end, and there were some large margins of uncertainty which remained. The experiments demonstrated the extreme rigidity inherent to the geometry of these surfaces. They were "PH" (or hyperbolic parabolics). It is essential that the S-curve be well chosen, meaning an S-curve which is sufficiently isolated from the layout. I then thought that it was absolutely necessary to use this geometric property as the surface structure and, from there, create a city, not in an obelisk form or a skyscraper, such as we see here in Paris or in the United States, but one in a continuous S-curve form. These are pellicles in space with a width of one hundred or one hundred and fifty meters, perforated, of course, and transparent, which would insure ventilation and visibility, light, etc. And there are already cities at an altitude of two thousand meters in Mexico and Bogotá. Therefore, it's a completely habitable altitude. Of course, it is different at five thousand meters, since the rarification of air becomes critical. No one really knows what happens. But with present technology, it is possible to obtain sufficient pressurization as well as temperature control and air renewal, such as in airplanes. After all, a city such as this one would simply be like stretching a garment. Man has not known clothing for a very long time. He has worn clothes for only about ten thousand years, no more. Before, he was nude. He later put on individualized, personalized garments. He works from morning to night in places such as we are right now, for example, which have no air and from where he cannot see the light of day. Most people work like that in offices and factories. This environment can be very nasty to man's health, and I think with present technology and the technology of the immediate future, these problems will be resolved in such a manner that everyone will be dressed for the city itself, allowing for a greater physical, conceptual, mental and spiritual freedom for man. This merely implies an extrapolation of today's technical possibilities, exploited on a larger scale. A city such as I propose is not conceivable under a restrained capitalistic system. It could be realized, though, by multinational companies or by centralized states (such as France, for example) which could build them but while avoiding a municipality system. Only a country with several tens of millions of inhabitants or even a sort of international corporation which could construct units of this type could consider such a program, which would be valid for either deserted or extremely cold regions such as Siberia, Alaska, or Northern Canada.

MICHEL RAGON

Aren't there any energy constraints which make the idea of heating such a volume seem difficult?

IANNIS XENAKIS

It's linked, of course, to energy problems. But we now have products and insulation systems which could reduce much of the thermal and caloric waste. I really don't think that the technical obstacles are real obstacles. The greatest obstacles fall under two catagories. First of all, there's the question of organization, since a city is an organization . . .

MICHEL RAGON

I was getting to that. I was going to say, precisely, that you must envision electronic management and decision-making groups in order to organize such a vertical city. In Nicolas Schoffer's "cybernetic city," though, we also find this belief in cybernetics and electronic management and decision-making groups. Don't you practice a belief which, to me, seems to be a dangerous one with regard to the political virtues of science? This occasionally comes across in your writings, by the way.

IANNIS XENAKIS

I don't know what Nicolas Schoffer said exactly. I believe he's rather mystical about cybernetics . . .

MICHEL RAGON

Yes, he goes further than you: it really does become a kind of mysticism, in fact.

IANNIS XENAKIS

We must recognize that, for the time being, data or management systems are rather rudimentary and vulgar. Only a few tasks could presently be undertaken and controlled by automatic management. But there are some which do work. For example, city traffic lights are becoming more and more automated, due to reactions and counterreactions from street to street, from neighborhood to neighborhood; that's a fact.

MICHEL RAGON

But this automation is almost always repressive.

IANNIS XENAKIS

We are faced with two problems: the problem of organization, and then, a deeper problem in that it's a problem of social structure. When I say organization, it's obvious that a city like this, which must comprise millions of individuals and at a five thousand-meter altitude, cannot be entirely conceived in advance because one risks creating a dead city. This was the case with Detroit, with le Havre, Brasilia, and even Chandigarh. They do not work because they were conceived in the laboratory—I mean, in architects' studios—following certain rules stemming from drawing board traditions, or even occasionally, from revolutionary ideas. They cannot take into consideration the whole comp exity of a city because of the simple fact that they have stemmed from one single brain. On the contrary, it is possible to give the framework (meaning the container) and not define or determine the contents. This would allow a freedom sufficiently great so that the contents could develop progressively. It must be understood that this sort of city could not be put up in five or even ten years, but could take up to twenty or thirty years to construct. Therefore, it's not the city itself which would be designed in advance, in twenty or thirty years, but the "container"; in other words, the fundamental structure which must be built up to this altitude. On the other hand, it

55

would be necessary to allow for improvements, if not developments, if not contradictions, which would progressively occur during the construction of this city. Consequently, it's absolutely necessary to conceive of a kind of mobile architecture. A hint of that idea can be found in Japanese architecture, which allows for the transformation of rooms or houses following diversified functions.

MICHEL RAGON

Internal nomadism is possible thanks to the permutations of the architecture's mobility, as you accurately point out.

IANNIS XENAKIS

I haven't spoken of internal nomadism yet; I simply spoke of nomadism, let's say of the city's physical aspect. This is to say that we can assign this or that function to an area or region of the city, let's say a factory, and then change these functions into dwellings or a park, etc. after a while. It's a question of the internal structure mobility within the physical city. As for the second and more difficult obstacle, human dwellings and functions within this container: it's absolutely necessary to leave freedom or to propose a sufficiently free schema which would insure an autonomous development in this domain so that the contradictions can be displaced, can change form. (I don't say that they will be cancelled or absorbed; this can't happen. It's a utopia which dates back to the nineteenth century, if not earlier.)

MICHEL RAGON

You also write, "Since this city, your city will be fashioned following universal technique, it will be equally apt to house populations from the great north or south, from the tropics, and from the deserts." In other words, it seems to me that a dangerous technocratic belief in a universal or typical man appears in this text. It's a very widespread idea. It can be found in Le Corbusier, as well as Gropius. And since there is a universal, "typical" man, architects deduce that a typical and universal architecture can be constructed for this man: a belief we've strayed away from a bit these days.

IANNIS XENAKIS

Yes, it's just that technology imposes a certain universality, but I wonder if we have really strayed away from this idea or whether only in spirit. If you consider to what extent technological means have spread . . . all the way to the heart of the most primitive societies, with electricity, with different sorts of energy and energy transformations but also with institutions which means that now, there are schools, universities, and textbooks everywhere you look. The scientific textbooks and laboratories are the same, the clothing is the same, even if they are different on the historical level. It is rare now to find people dressed in their national costume, a fact which is due to a general universalization, caused by all sorts of reasons. On the other hand, I am not a technocrat, far from it. On the contrary, I don't mean to say, though, that present technology should not be used and exploited. There are at least two aspects to every proposition: the black and the white. It's the same for atomic energy. It's an incredible miracle that man has been able to see and enter into the microcosmos of matter and subsequently take advantage of what he finds there. It's also absolutely normal to now find deviations since this is part of man's nature, it's one of man's inherent contradictions, and it's also a question of individual and social struggle.

MICHEL RAGON

Finally, one last question: how do you situate yourself as an architect, since you are still an architect, seeing that you have invented an architecture for the esplanade at the George Pompidou center* in Paris (which is destined to be very closely associated with music) which will, without a doubt, be a Polytope and in which there will be music?You have also recently constructed a private home for the musician François-Bernard Mâche. How do you situate yourself in relation to your former employer, Le Corbusier, who is highly objected to these days by many of your colleagues and by many architectural theoreticians?

IANNIS XENAKIS

First, in relation to architecture . . . When I decided to do only music, I was very distressed because architecture was very important to me. I did it because I had to make a choice. Either go into research or become a businessman. In the sixties, I went to architects' studios and said, "Here I am! Let me introduce myself

---

*Xenakis' *Diatope* (at Georges Pompidou Arts Center) within which was played "La Legende d'Eer," 46 minutes of sound and light action (1600 electronic flashes, 4 laser beams, 400 mirrors, miscellaneous optical devices plus 7-track tape). (Trans. note).

as an architect who would like to collaborate, but I don't want to be someone's slave; I want to do research." That was impossible. You know very well that this is true the majority of the time and that there are very few opportunities to do architectural research. I therefore confined myself to music where, despite all the difficulties, I could devote myself to artistic research. All this said and done, I'm always ready to do architecture whenever I can. For example, for this "thingamajig" at Beaubourg, I designed a portable structure which will be installed for several months and will house the means to put on a *spectacle* with lasers and electronic flashes, like at Cluny,* only more elaborate. And the structure is a cloth structure,** which therefore implies some fundamental architectural solutions. On the other hand, in relation to Le Corbusier, I don't know if there are many other architects who have achieved what I consider to be artistic expression. Independent of an architect's or urbanist's subjacent ideas, this is something very complex which comes from different sources and directions. The cellular apartment included the Marseille project can be contested, of course, and is but one possible solution. It cannot be said that it's the only solution. Besides, Le Corbusier proved this himself since he designed all types of houses. On the contrary, his artistic and architectural qualities, which are demonstrated in practically all of his works, cannot be contested. Ideas move on, but artistic fact remains. It's one of history's lessons, as Marx himself noted with regard to antique art. Approximately, he said or asked how is it that, at the rim of civilization and western culture in spite of slave societies, etc., works were created which still affect us today? It's a miracle inherent to artistic fact and corresponds to the discussion earlier, to the question which Olivier Messaien and Revault d'Allonnes asked. Therefore, Le Corbusier can be criticized on a lot of points; I even do it myself, but I believe he was one of the greatest architects of our time. There are not thirty-six of them today, perhaps there isn't even one.

---

*"Polytope de Cluny," a sound and light show, 24 minutes for 7- or 4-track tape, 600 electronic flashes, 3 laser beams, optical devices, fixed or mobile mirrors. The music is to be broadcast over 12 loudspeakers and the whole operation is cóntrolled by computer-calculated numeric tape which is simultaneously decoded for each "performance." This work was presented during the "Paris Contemporary Music Days" in 1972 at the Cluny Museum for 6 months (4 performances per day). 90,000 people were able to share this event.

** The *Diatope* is constructed with a waterproof canvas. (trans. note)

MICHEL RAGON

I have no more questions, and since I quibbled with you a little about technocracy, I would not like to omit pointing out that, in all of your texts, there is an eulogy to art. Such praise of art is so uncommon and remarkable today, when we hear mostly about the death of art. Also, your definition of the artist-conceptor seems to me to be of major importance. In all of your texts, one acknowledges your intelligence and also what you call that "cold fire," not about you yourself, but in relation to the manner by which you could be accused of working. I've always seen you a bit like a "cold fire." This has always fascinated me, both in your music and your architecture. Because of the very fervent admiration I have for you, I consider it a great honor to be here today, not to judge you, but to welcome you.

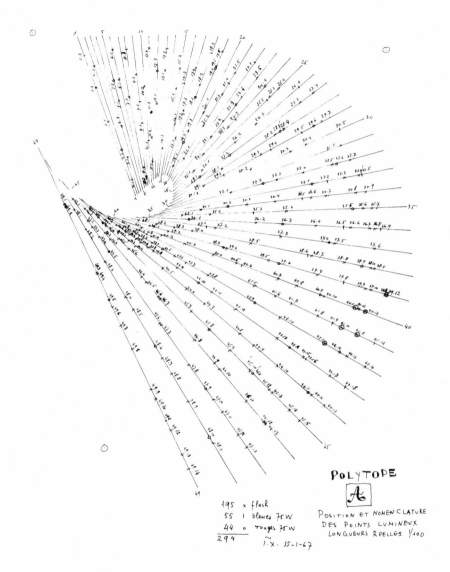

Fig. 5. Polytope A of the *Polytope de Montréal.*

DIALOGUE WITH
MICHEL SERRES

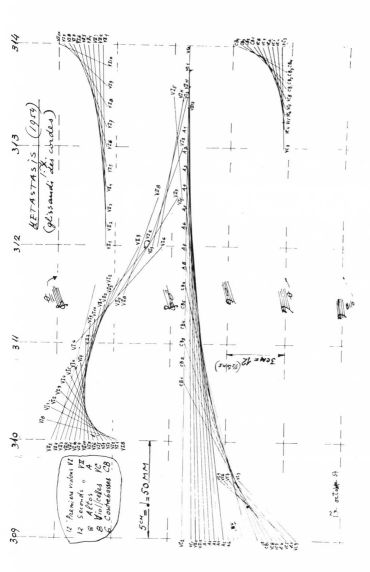

Fig. 6. Diagram of the glissandi by the strings in *Metastasis*. Each instrument is assigned its own individual part. The first instance in the history of music of achieving the effect of mass through the use of organized glissandi.

Xenakis remarked on the interrelation between musical glissandi and the laws of geometry. Start-ing with this observation, he worked out the ruled surfaces of the Philips Pavilion. The thought carried over from music to architecture; hence the affinity between this document and the Philips Pavilion or the cable structures of Montreal does not occur by chance.

BERNARD TEYSSÈDRE
Now I'd like to give the floor to Michel Serres.

MICHEL SERRES
I don't think that space is the image of society only in architecture. For example, today, there is an admirer behind this table and an inventor in front of it; it's not my fault if this is the University's image. The University is partial to theses and not to works, creative outputs. Since for once we have a creative output rather than a thesis before us, it is with much admiration that I would like to praise this phenomenon which is so rare within the general waste of intelligence which occurs in institutions. Hence, it is an admirer who will be asking the questions. Later, we will come back to the relationships between mathematics and music. On page 14* of the thesis presentation you proposed the global idea of a general morphology when speaking of the artist-conceptor. What is this general morphology?

IANNIS XENAKIS
Well, in every domain of human activity, form exists as a sort of froth. I have noticed some figures, some forms, which belong to either the domain of abstract speculation (such as mathematics, logic), or to more concrete speculation (such as physics , treating either atomic or subatomic phenomena), or to geometrical expressions of genetics (such as chemical molecular reactions).

*Page 5 of this translation.

63

Yet these figures, these forms which belong to so many dissimilar domains also have fascinating similarities and diversifications and can enlighten other domains such as artistic activities.

MICHEL SERRES

When did you write that? Recently?

IANNIS XENAKIS

Oh! I don't know, a few years ago.

MICHEL SERRES

Two questions or subquestions. At the end of the paragraph near the end of the article where you introduce this general morphology, you use the example of the formal evolution of vertebrates.

IANNIS XENAKIS

Vertebrates, yes, that's one example.

MICHEL SERRES

It is a very good example. Someone before Xenakis also had this idea of a general morphology, but in biology. Geoffroy Saint-Hilaire had the idea of a general layout which could be projected onto the whole of vertebrates and then, more generally, onto the whole of the animal kingdom. But, at present, there is someone else who is dealing with this idea of general morphology in such a way that your idea of morphogenesis coincides with an aspect of science already at work; I mean Reví Thom. As usual, the musician took the lead.

IANNIS XENAKIS

All the better! It would also be necessary for Thom to be fluent in the artistic domain and not only in physics. But I believe that this same idea has a much earlier antecedent, under another form.

MICHEL SERRES

I believe Geoffroy was the first, wasn't he?

IANNIS XENAKIS

I don't know. I believe this idea can be traced back to antiquity; for example, when the idea of proportion was first applied to architecture on man-made forms. This is a case of local morphology.

MICHEL SERRES

This local morphology is not the same thing as Xenakis' idea of general morphology.

IANNIS XENAKIS

But I think it's indispensible to create a kind of convergence of all possible forms, from all sides which would presuppose a knowledge of these different sciences.

MICHEL SERRES

Was there a mathematical framework at the base of your project for this kind of morphology?

IANNIS XENAKIS

Oh no! Not at all . . .

MICHEL SERRES

Topology?

IANNIS XENAKIS

Topology? Topology, from what point of view? Because if topology is the most fundamental science in the mathematical realm . . .

MICHEL SERRES

Certainly, with regard to forms.

IANNIS XENAKIS

With regard to forms, but not only forms; also, to the philosophical thinking behind mathematics, don't you think? It's a problem of continuity, discontinuity, contacts and connectedness.

MICHEL SERRES

Borders.

IANNIS XENAKIS

Yes, borders, and consequently, forms. Topology is probably the subadjacent tool, though I think it's still rather crude at this time. It's too imperfect to tackle problems as complex as cloud formations or population forms.

MICHEL SERRES

But the idea of general morphology began precisely when dealing with problems such as cloud formations. As for your first appendix on the list of coincidences between musical and mathematical developments,* I agree with you and I would like only to add to it. When you say that before our era there was something like a comparative analysis between string lengths and pitches, I suppose your were referring to Pythagoras and the Pythagorean school. Today, the conviction that there was no analogy between the first musical intervals and mathematical invention is more and more frequent. It is now thought that it's more a question of cause and effect, meaning that thanks to music, the idea of a group of natural numbers, as well as fractions and relationships, was developed. If this was the case, music would have been the matrix of mathematical invention.

IANNIS XENAKIS

Yes, this is an archeological problem.

MICHEL SERRES

Once again, musical thinking is in the forefront. What do you mean when you say that the fugue is an automaton, that "the fugue is an abstract automaton conceived two centuries before automated science?" I don't believe this is true. I think they coincided, if science didn't appear first.

IANNIS XENAKIS

Oh no, not automated science. Automated science was born in the 20th century.

MICHEL SERRES

Not automated science, but the construction of automatons.

IANNIS XENAKIS

That makes a difference, because the use of automatons dates from Alexandrian times.

MICHEL SERRES

In *A Thousand and One Nights,* for example, there are automatic fountains, water machines.

*cf. Appendix I, p. 99.

IANNIS XENAKIS

Yes, but *A Thousand and One Nights* dates from the 12th century, but the use of automatons occurs much earlier than that. The Alexandrian period already knew Heron and the first steam machine.

MICHEL SERRES

Yes, even Archytus' dove.

IANNIS XENAKIS

All of these are concrete inventions. It was music, I believe, which introduced its abstraction.

MICHEL SERRES

So then, why is the fugue an automaton?

IANNIS XENAKIS

I think that it corresponds more or less to the definition of a scientific automaton which came about in the twenties thanks to Wiener and cybernetics. It can be summarized in the following manner: An automaton is a network of causes and effects, meaning a temporal chain of events, eventually coupled or multicoupled with certain liberties. An automaton can be closed. It suffices to plug in energy and it works cyclically. It can be relatively open, complete with data entries and external actions, thanks to the help of buttons, for example. Every time new data entries are given, an automaton can produce different results, despite the internal rigor which defines it.

MICHEL SERRES

Its syntaxes are repetative but not its performances.

IANNIS XENAKIS

Yes, its syntaxes are repetitive. Why? Because there is an internal structural rigor.

MICHEL SERRES

Is the fugue's syntax always stable?

IANNIS XENAKIS

The fugue does not constitute such an absolute automaton; it is a relative automaton, especially when compared to the automatons studied by science, which are relatively rigorous in relation to musical ones. When I say musical automaton, I consider that a minuet is also an automaton. The value specific to musical invention is that it was the first to give ,to create an abstract automaton, meaning that it produced nothing at all except music.

MICHEL SERRES

Is time in this music reversible or not?

IANNIS XENAKIS

Well, there, the problem is one of time in general, whereas here, there's a sort of confusion in the minds of most men, including musicians. The fact that things can be repeated, experiences or phenomena renewed, offers them a kind of security with regard to time, which, in fact, never repeats itself.

MICHEL SERRES

Sometimes we encounter reversible time.

IANNIS XENAKIS

Which time is reversible?

MICHEL SERRES

Planetary movement.

IANNIS XENAKIS

Time is not reversible; it's time's movement which is reversible. Time itself (to my knowledge, it's a kind of postulate) or the temporal flow never goes backwards.

MICHEL SERRES

In any case, this is a very recent discovery.

IANNIS XENAKIS

That time never goes backwards?

MICHEL SERRES

Absolutely.

IANNIS XENAKIS

But it's so natural to think that it doesn't go backwards. Heraclitus said the same thing, by the way. There could eventually be a reversability of time if the universe's movement were pendular meaning that it would contract and dilate. For example, when I talk about time intervals, they are commutative. This is to say that I can take time intervals now or later and commutate them with other time intervals. But the individual instants which make up these time intervals are not reversible, they are absolute, meaning that they belong to time, which means that there is something which escapes us entirely since time runs on. This corresponds to the research Piaget did while experimentally observing the phases of childrens' apprenticeship in time.

MICHEL SERRES

What I have in mind is Xenakis and not Piaget.

IANNIS XENAKIS

Ah!

MICHEL SERRES

Yes, when you come along with compositions based on stochastics, that touches upon the problem of time.

IANNIS XENAKIS

Yes.

MICHEL SERRES

When composing, what relations do you draw between order and disorder?

IANNIS XENAKIS

Order and disorder?

MICHEL SERRES

I know what disorder is because I know how you handle that. But what is order, what is your syntax?

IANNIS XENAKIS

Well, there are several facets. For example, I can say there's order when there's symmetry.

MICHEL SERRES

That's it; already, with symmetry, we've won.

IANNIS XENAKIS

Yes, there you've won, of course. But it's not a question of winning; it's a question of vocabulary.

MICHEL SERRES

No. No, I've won, so that means we're going to come back to the question of time. If there is symmetry there can be reversability . . .

IANNIS XENAKIS

No, because there can be order in non-temporal things. That's why it's absolutely indispensible to distinguish between what is *in* and what is *outside* of time. For example, I'll take a group of keys on a piano (an elementary case). I then have intervals which repeat themselves, but they are never repeated in time; they're there, fixed. The piano keys are on a piano which doesn't move.

MICHEL SERRES

Therefore these keys are outside of time?

IANNIS XENAKIS

Yes, outside of time.

MICHEL SERRES

The syntax is outside time?

IANNIS XENAKIS

Yes.

MICHEL SERRES

I suspected that!

IANNIS XENAKIS

There, I have symmetries because I have relationships; therefore, I have repetitions.

MICHEL SERRES

Yes. Then order is outside of time?

IANNIS XENAKIS

There are some orders which can be outside of time. Now, if I apply this idea to time, I can still obtain these orders, but not in real time, meaning in the temporal flow, because this flow is never reversible. I can obtain them in a fictitious time which is based on memory.

MICHEL SERRES

Is the piano a recollection?

IANNIS XENAKIS

Yes, it is a concrete recollection.

MICHEL SERRES

A concrete recollection. The question then would be the following: Can you obtain an irreversible flow?

IANNIS XENAKIS

Of course I can, since I'm not a gas, and at the same time I'm possessed by Maxwell's demon.*

MICHEL SERRES

Maxwell's demon puts things in order.

IANNIS XENAKIS

Maxwell's demon can reverse things.

MICHEL SERRES

Now we're getting there. So, there are reversible structures in music.

IANNIS XENAKIS

They are reversible outside time.

MICHEL SERRES

Would Maxwell's demon go on outside of time?

---

*In the case of complete disorder, Maxwell's formula, as applied to two dimensions, enables us to calculate the probability $f(v)$ of the existence of a rector r on a given plane: $f(v) = \dfrac{2r}{a2} e^{-v2/a2}$. (trans. note)

IANNIS XENAKIS

I chose Maxwell's demon, but this demon doesn't change the order of the temporal flow itself. You must understand what happens. For example, when a flow of light is said to give lasers, laser light (after having gone through certain conditions and therefore having become organized and orderly), well, it's as if Maxwell's demon intervened within. Because otherwise, we would have had just any disorderly light. But this applies exclusively to notions or beings which, by definition, could be reversible. Time itself is not reversible; I insist upon that.

MICHEL SERRES

Xenakis, if anyone, has proven that. The drift from order or structure to disorder is one of your compositional secrets. Do you agree?

IANNIS XENAKIS

Yes.

MICHEL SERRES

The first proposed theorem in physics was about vibrating strings. Isn't a vibrating string a reversible phenomenon?

IANNIS XENAKIS

Outside time positions are reversible.

MICHEL SERRES

What do you call outside-time positions? I don't understand.

IANNIS XENAKIS

Spatial intervals, for example, string positions. They are reversible because they belong to space, which is not temporal.

MICHEL SERRES

Therefore it's a clock!

IANNIS XENAKIS

Therefore it's a clock.

MICHEL SERRES

In fact, a clock, like a vibrating string, counts time. A vibrating string can be a time index. It's measurement.

IANNIS XENAKIS

It's a time index which is based not on time, but on the reversibility of positions. This is the fundamental idea. As Heraclitus said, no one can live the same instant twice. Someone tried to prove the reversibility of time about 15 years ago using the idea of parity in microphysics (no one has demonstrated this yet) but we don't have the experimental data . . .

MICHEL SERRES

The kinds of music in question are an attempt to fight against temporal irreversibility?

IANNIS XENAKIS

If you wish.

MICHEL SERRES

We're going to be able to generalize on this topic little by little and move on from technique to composition. Is there a relationship between glissandi and the aforesaid irreversibility? This seems to me to be a very important point. You'll see why later.

IANNIS XENAKIS

I don't know whether the glissando is in direct relation to this or not.

MICHEL SERRES

You do agree that the glissando is an important element in your composition?

IANNIS XENAKIS

Yes.

MICHEL SERRES

Why did you chose the glissando?

IANNIS XENAKIS

Perhaps it's an influence from Euclidian geometry. Perhaps because the glissando is precisely a modification of something in time, but imperceptible, meaning that it is continuous but can't be grasped because man is a discontinuous being. Not only is he discontinuous in his perceptions and judgments, but in everything. Continuity is something which constantly escapes him. It's a

Zenonian problematic or simply a change in itself and it's a sort of perpetual fight to try to imagine continuous movement in our perceptions and judgments. This is what happened especially in mathematics by the way. The maths first started with the discontinuous only to end up with continuity much later.

MICHEL SERRES

There are two elements in your work which make me think of irreversibility. The first is the drifting from order to disorder by way of probability functions, and the second is the consistently used glissando element.

IANNIS XENAKIS

Yes.

MICHEL SERRES

Then, Xenakis' music no longer corresponds to the definition of a fight against irreversibility which was stated earlier since you accept irreversibility in these two fundamental techniques. Isn't your music different than all others specifically in that it has admitted, once and for all, the irreversibility of time? As opposed to any other music.

IANNIS XENAKIS

I'll have to get back to that because I don't believe in the reversibility of time, of real, immediate time, the temporal flow. I think that it's impossible to make time go backwards.

MICHEL SERRES

Yes, so it is.

IANNIS XENAKIS

Therefore, time is irreversible. Judgments which are made in the time flow are, if you please, reversible. As an example, let's take the most elementary thing there is: durations. A duration is something that can be moved about within time, it is therefore reversible, commutative. A duration always occurs in the same direction as time, of course (it can go against the temporal flow). This is to say that if I want to write, design, or, especially, visually represent time, I would have to put it on an axis, as physicists do, as musicians do (first musicians, and later, physicists). It must be pointed out that musicians with the musical staff were the first to invent a

Cartesian representation of this principle. Fine. The temporal flow would be represented by a straight line which, by definition, would be a continuity. I'll put points on this line: these are instants. The difference between any two points is a concept which stems from comparisons and mysterious judgments I make about the reality of the temporal flow, which I accept *a priori.* The distance between the two points is what is then identified as a duration. I displace this duration anywhere; therefore, it is reversible. But the temporal flow itself is irreversible. And if I draw an axis on a spatial plane and place pitches on it, on an axis perpendicular to an horizontal time axis, then, to go from a low point to a higher point to the right of it, I can only move in one way: from bottom to top, and from left to right. That's irreversibility.

MICHEL SERRES

We have reached the notion of irreversibility which characterizes your music by two technical methods: on the one hand, by the drifting from order to disorder and, on the other hand, by the use of glissandi. What also strikes me, generally speaking, in both your music and your architecture and which is another invariant of your vision of the world, is ruled surfaces, meaning PH, hyperboloides, etc. Why such persistence on ruled surfaces?

IANNIS XENAKIS

For many reasons, I believe.

MICHEL SERRES

Be very careful about answering because this is exactly the contrary to what was said earlier. Earlier, there was the drifting toward chance, whereas if we start from this insistence on ruled surfaces, there is a renewal of repetitive structures.

IANNIS XENAKIS

Yes, this is another kind of preoccupation. It's a problem of continuity and discontinuity stemming from linear elements. A line is perhaps the most basic element of continuity, of an expression of continuity.

MICHEL SERRES

Isn't it merely the result of a framing technique? Because it's easier to frame off ruled surfaces.

IANNIS XENAKIS

No, it's impossible to frame them off since they are S-curves; it would be necessary to . . .

MICHEL SERRES

Yes, it's possible. Since the surfaces are ruled, you necessarily have frameworks made up of ever-straight planes on a PH or a hyperboloide.

IANNIS XENAKIS

Yes, but since it's with S-curves, space is distorted, and the ordinary framework made up of flat planes would adopt S-curves only very imperfectly. If it were necessary to construct a "warped" framework, as for boats for example, it would cost much too much.

MICHEL SERRES

Let's get back to ruled surfaces and the situation which they've allowed us . . . a ruled surface can be developed from straight lines.

IANNIS XENAKIS

Yes, there's something absolutely fascinating about a straight line. A ray of sunlight is fascinating in itself. Rays of sunlight can be seen when looked at through clouds. The rays of sun which converge near the ground are, in reality, parallels. A laser's beam line is something absolute, the line of a mason's edge is also absolute. The straight line, therefore, exists in nature. But as an intellectual entity, it's most fascinating from the point of view of speed, direction, and also continuity. From the point of view of continuity, it's impossible to imagine anything simpler than a straight line. Because once you have a curve, for example, you can imagine the forces which produced it, and there are all sorts of torsions and rich curves, while a straight line is one, without forces, identically repeating itself. Excuse me, I haven't finished yet with ruled surfaces. Ruled surfaces are developed from straight lines in three dimensions (the glissando being a two-dimensional line). The straight line enables us to imagine very complex forms with very simple and controllable elements.

MICHEL SERRES

Minimum of techniques, maximum of realizations . . .

IANNIS XENAKIS

Of results.

MICHEL SERRES

Yes, all right . . . The final question will be the following (I'll stop here): in the beginning of your book (*Formalized Music*), you have yet another bone to pick with data processors, but it's nevertheless necessary to distinguish between data processing and information theory.

IANNIS XENAKIS

The good guys and the bad guys!

MICHEL SERRES

Finally, when we speak of disorder, it has to do with thermodynamic disorder, but it also has to do with background noise. Consequently, they are the same thing. Here's the last question: there are two things concerning Xenakis that I can't put together. First, there is a sort of fascination for ruled invariants (in other words, ruled surfaces) and then, for syntactical invariants, and following suit, invariance in general; in sum, repetitive syntax. Second, there is a fascination which indicates your thermodynamic preoccupations, for background noise, etc., and the glissandi which are elements of this; in other words, the inverse preoccupation, the preoccupation to "gliss" or slide irreversibly toward disorder, toward background noise. How do you account for this unvarying fascination for syntax and this fascination for this drifting toward disorder? Can music be defined as such?

IANNIS XENAKIS

No, because disorder is a negation of order (which here means repetition). Disorder, then (in the periodic sense) is reversible, of course. (Something periodic is reversible, but by its own definition). What I mean by this is that what is not temporal by essence is reversible. Beings can position themselves in any order in this domain which is, by definition, outside time. It's this constant preoccupation with these two poles, with order or disorder, personified by periodicity (he who says periodicity, also says invariant); it's the whole scale of possible levels which, in my opinion, constitutes a sort of mental category. This is what can be found throughout all of history and philosophy as well as science, and which is one of the subjacent preoccupations in my music.

MICHEL SERRES

One last corollary question: Starting from noise, can there be order?

IANNIS XENAKIS

Yes. And then what's interesting is that we can simulate noises, which is, physically speaking, a pressure variation that never renews itself identically. It can be fabricated either with cathodic tubes or by calculating machines. Yet the listener goes one step beyond. he doesn't stay at the lower level of the specimen's microscopically individual event, and he perceives noise as a macroscopically individual whole; in other words, as something possessing a regularity, an order!

MICHEL SERRES

So, the answer can now be given; it is perfectly general. You know that all the questions which have just been asked revolve around the problem: Can order be established from noise? Well, your music was the first to discover this.

IANNIS XENAKIS

Thank you so very much.

DIALOGUE WITH
BERNARD TEYSSÈDRE

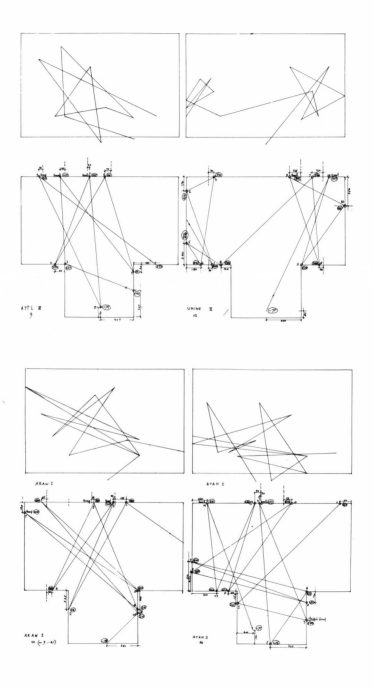

Fig. 7.   Cluny 2. Elevations and planes of the laser
configurations.

BERNARD TEYSSÈDRE

Well, since the moment has come to conclude this defense and since habit (or protocol) leaves the last words to the jury's president, please allow me, dear Iannis Xenakis, to express my joy and excitement at seeing you present this thesis.

First of all, for personal reasons. I'll never forget your surprise and even skepticism when I suggested to you a few years ago that you should apply to the U. E. R.* for an associate professorship at the Plastic Arts and the Science of Art School, where I was then director. Within this new framework you progressively built up a pedagogical idea which has become your graduate and postgraduate seminars: "Formalization and Programming in the Visual Arts and Music." Neither will I forget your surprise when, in agreement with our mutual friend Olivier Revault d'Allonnes, I suggested that you present a dissertation for a *doctorat d'Etat*,† bringing together the scores and texts we are discussing today.

Here, the personal reasons arouse the same questions of principle which Michel Serres brought up earlier. Like him, I'm pleased that high quality researchers can be granted the state doctorate, regardless of the fact that their career and training have nothing "Sorbonne-ish" about them. For a while now, this practice has

---

*Unités d'Etudes et de Recherches: a special department in French universities which is strictly devoted to advanced research. (trans. note)

†In the hierarchy of the French National Education System, this is the highest degree attainable. (Trans. note).

been accepted in foreign universities, especially in America; nevertheless, in France this is brand new. I remember the incredulity I encountered, even in 1969–70, when defending the mere idea that a musician or sculptor could have his place next to a learned history or philosophy professor at the Sorbonne. The university is not made for artists, they objected. And why not? Since then, it seems to me that they've gone straight for it. There are no longer only programs in musicology, filmography, and art history, but also now, music, cinema, and plastic art programs are in effect where theory and practice are combined.

Artistic application is no longer practiced for the sole benefit of reflective theorization, as it has been even up until the recent past. This type of discourse is often relegated to history's hegemony. But, in less than five years, university programs, complete with artistic subjects, have been put into use, from the first cycle to the various diplomas, to masters' degrees, from IPES to the CAPES and to the "agrégation."* Personalities such as Michel Butor, Maurice Lemaître, Georges Charbonnier, and Frank Popper today have their state doctorates. A fresco painter such as José Balmès or a theatre man such as Jacques Clancy teach their art as associate conference masters, and this present defense registers its fullest meaning from this perspective.

Your dissertation, dear Xenakis, is a *real* dissertation, in the most sanctified meaning of the word—almost in its medieval sense. It is so in that first, it avoids the snag of other defenses or "file-dissertations": it is by no means a haphazard collection of incongruous works. On the contrary, it distinguishes itself by a profound unity since the presented texts, along with their accompanying scores, converge around the same fundamental theme and this theme has been the basis of much of today's debate: the alloys (and not a "marriage") between the arts and sciences.

Would this not more likely refer to *one certain* conception of art? And *one certain* conception of science? I admit that this is what I believe. But it's specifically because of this that your dissertation is *really* a dissertation, in a second way: it is not an erudite re-

---

*The state-supported system of higher education in France is divided into "cycles." Upon completion of any given cycle, a diploma is awarded. Furthermore, there are nation-wide competitions by which "competitors" or students qualify for varying positions in the French public service sector, including teaching. The most competitive of these competitions is the "agregation" which is roughly equivalent to an American Ph.D. (Trans. note).

search report on some little point (as is often the case), but an original theory, and consequently arguable and even contestable—once again as during the Middle Ages when the "doctors" confronted each other around Duns Scotus or William of Occam.

I would like to examine this one point, however briefly, so as not to delay the conclusion of this already rather long session. Using only one of the written works in your file, I would like to bring into light the other side of the *latent hypotheses* which subtend your dissertation. These form the coherence and define the *philosophical option* of your work: an entirely personal option, validated by this same coherence. Perhaps I'm mistaken, Xenakis, but it seems to me that yours is one option among others which could be different, if not contradictory, though neither more nor less valid than others. I'm going to raise a few objections to that which underlies (or what seems to me to underlie) the perhaps unperceived or unacknowledged group of underlying hypotheses which are the basis of your dissertation. I specify ahead of time that I will not handle all the objections (at least in their extreme form). Nevertheless, it seems to me that one of the rules of the game is to play the "devil's advocate," so as to instigate your reactions, and your counterattack with the hope that you will be able to clarify your own point of view. And then to proceed to the extremities to better appreciate how and how much *your* point of view is *your own.* This will help me to dissipate the uneasiness I am weak enough to feel when confronted by any aesthetic theory which claims to be universally valid and will also help me to eliminate the hints of "cultural imperialism" I'd be likely to suspect from it.

I'll say this on the subject: I found a major advantage in your work *Formalized Music* which would be comparable to axiomatics in Hilber's or Paeno's meaning, and that is to found music on the basis of certain generalities through the annexing of the restrictive constraints which would determine them so that specific types of music (not all) could be deduced as partial ensembles. These constraints (which are, in other words, keys, modes, series, etc.) would determine the sonic universe which would then distinguish the fields of musical possibilities within. I did say *universe* and not *"pluriverse."* And I want to say that *Formalized Music* (though perhaps Xenakis' thinking has evolved since) seems to me to reason *as if* there were hope of an all-encompasing theory, covering the group of thinkable realms without a gap, *as if* Gödel's theorem could be surpassed and be more than merely shaped by procedural stratagems. I sense that Xenakis has opted in favor of a "system of the universe," and because of this, his thesis seems to be even more fundamental since it is really a *thesis*, agreeing with the conditions which have generated a large number of musical works. Nevertheless, your thesis allows for other theses to subsist alongside yours which would be capable of serving as the basis for other musical works. Leaving this general level, I'll get to more specific questions and attempt to show that Xenakis' theory entails at least two postulates and several options, some being methodological while others are clearly subjective.

The first postulate will be this: in *Formalized Music,* history and culture seem to be relegated to the background, leaving priority to research on logico-mathematical invariants. Perhaps Xenakis' musical theory would find certain conceptual equivalents in this regard to serial, or systematic or programmed painting. (For example, an inventory or "trick list" of Vasarely's optical effects.) However, I wonder if the hypothesis of stochastic distribution can really be defended when it entails absolute probabilistic equivalences at their starting points and in the course of their trajectories. On the contrary, the anatomy and embryology of higher vertebrates could show that the code of genetic determinations isn't all that "enriched" during the course of their evolution ("enriched" in the sense of "enriching" an information bank.) They could also show that the nervous system's development (especially the cortical centers) unveils itself mostly by a proliferation of neurons and by the relative instability of their synoptic connections. In other words, the most archaic mammals known to man (or the inventing of pre-established regulations) wouldn't be increased at all. It would even be significantly decreased if it's referred back to the multiplicity of networks, of possible connections. A sort of "aleatoric trailblazing" results, a guided aleatory : not because there is a lack of determinants, but because this inventory is governed by determinants other than genetic ones; in other words, because the role of apprenticeship tends to progressively deter pure and simple maturation. This apprenticeship is, moreover, conditioned by a context which could be qualified as being historical (in the most general sense of the word), starting from the intra-uterine stage and leading up to family life and scholastic situations, up to the sociocultural environment.

You wonder what I'm getting at? This: the inference between pre-established elements, including formalizable invariants (those which Xenakis formalizes) on the one hand, and, on the other hand, a bundle of cultural and historical accidents which an individual man could not dismiss. It seems to me that this must be taken into account. In relation to the genetic inventory, or "chance" series, in the most banal sense (that of Counot), this inference constituted an intersection of independant causal chains. And what makes this chance series a continuous guided chain instead of an erratic dispersion is that it is permanently stowed away in a relatively constant sociocultural context. I wonder whether it is possible under these conditions to maintain (as Xenakis does many times in his book) the fiction about *amnesia*? Is it advantageous to consider man as being "amnesiac," to pinpoint him the instant his perceptions occur, by abstracting his individual past? Or, on the contrary, is it not necessary to admit that a purely stochastic distribution is nearly excluded from the musical realm since there would be no probability equivalences either at the starting points or in the trajectories? In other words, is it possible to isolate the logico-mathematical invariants, as if a musical experience did not integrate determinants of different orders such as sociocultural or historical ones? Is my question clear, Xenakis?

IANNIS XENAKIS

Perhaps, I don't know.

BERNARD TEYSSÈDRE

What I mean to say is that the sociocultural conditioning wouldn't be only an extension of something which itself would be added on to the probabilities that are considered as being initially equiprobable, but on the contrary, the networks themselves of relationships would constitute it. And all this in such a manner that we could never start from a sort of absolute "no man's land," from a "clean sweep," but on the contrary, from a highly stratified terrain.

IANNIS XENAKIS

Yes, but this "highly stratified" is not at all proven. It is precisely one of the fundamental subjects of research in all domains. In biology or genetics, for example, very little is known about the heredity of more or less elaborated and complex mental structures. It's a hereditory fact which establishes that we are not plants or minerals. We are men who, moreover, resemble one another, with eyes, with organs. But the one place where we have no idea what's going on is *there,* in our brain's constitution, since we don't know heredity's role in what we could call "categories." We don't know how the principle of causality was born or why it was born. Moreover, this principle is equivalent to referential reasoning. Furthermore, the meaning we give to time, to the temporal flow depends not only on experience but also on our brain's concrete constructions. We don't know when these constructions occur: is it after birth, or well before that, meaning thousands or millions of years ago. No one can decide. On the contrary, what we can eventually say is that there is indeed a nondetermined part within our mental structure. Why can we say that? Well, because there are so many cultures, so many approaches to reality, so many reactions before an objective universe (if such a thing exists!) This plurality enables greater freedom on the higher planes. Therefore, in this case, can't we change things which, at the moment, seem immutable and universal? Let's imagine the flow of time as we conceive it, including its orderly structure which is subjacent to our knowledge and which is part of our daily life, be we atomic physicists or musicians.

Is this concept of the time-flow absolute or could it be? In order to define these types of things and also to eliminate all the dust of education or sociocultural tradition, it's necessary to assume, to make perhaps rather extreme hypotheses from time to time, such as amnesia, for example. It's simply a work tool.

BERNARD TEYSSÈDRE

I was very surprised, Xenakis, when you referred to Greek music as being the nutritive humus from which our Western tradition has developed. I wonder if it isn't also the humus on and from which Xenakis' theory of a universal music has been founded. And I dare say, what Olivier Messiaen said about the possibilities of radically different structures from these does not contradict me. I'll remind you of my argument: given that genetic coding is extremely insufficient in relation to the multiplicity of synaptic connections between neurons, the trajectories are blazed in the course of their individual development, with these developments themselves being conditioned in large part by the sociocultural context. Why did a chord based on thirds, which was considered "dissonant" in the Middle Ages, become "consonant" in Bach's or Rameau's time, to the point that a major or minor third defined a "perfect chord" as being major or minor? My conclusion is that the postulate of initial equivalency between what is probable isn't, in fact, admissible, and to relegate the acculturalization or history of music to a secondary role merely to link it to logico-mathematical invariants, could be a very dangerous hypothesis. I'm not at all sure that we can just eliminate musical culture, not even with regards to sonic perception.

IANNIS XENAKIS

Well, if we climb up a ladder and look at history from a certain height, we'll see that a lot of things have happened. In order to see more clearly, it would be necessary to eliminate precisely these socio-cultural acquisitions. Once this is done, we could eventually find things which are independent from those, which are acquired or permanent, meaning time as well as space invariants. And that's why we suddenly find a "personality" which seems to be universal in the case of scales which changes only a bit throughout the world. This "personality" is the interval of a fourth. As if it were by chance, Aristoxenus starts his musical theory with this; he speaks of the perfect fourth. Nevertheless, he does not mathematically define this interval, because he does not reason as a Pythagorean, even though he knows mathematics and Pythagorism. But he does consider the perfect fourth as being the basic interval, and he begins his treatise with it. Moreover, we encounter the perfect fourth in all cultures throughout the world. On a higher level, it corresponds to a sort of musical invariant. But in order to understand, it's necessary to make a clean sweep of all the epipheno- mena, of all the specific colors of this or that musical culture, when we say that it's a sad, minor tonality or that it's in major. Obviously, this example is rather trivial. It's exactly the same on another level: when we say that music is melodic, must be melodic, must be polyphonic, and we can no longer conceive of any other music outside of this context. This also is a prejudice which comes to us from our socio-cultural conceptions. What must we do in order to get rid of all of that, in order to establish funda- mental thinking? The mathematicians and logicians of the nine- teenth century showed us one way when they got rid of verbal mathematics and replaced it with symbolic mathematics. And it is in this manner that I have tried to see more clearly.

BERNARD TEYSSÈDRE

That's what I said at the beginning; and that certainly is one sort of axiomatic open to us. Excuse me, I'm obliged to move on quickly because we don't have much time left and I still have a lot of questions to ask you. I'd like to leave this subject and go on to another point, another of your *postulates*, in my opinion: the one which could be called the principle of "composed dispersion."

When reading *Formalized Music* we could think that you allow for a precedence (at least a methodological one) of elements, let's say of sounds or particles or clouds of particles or logical classes, or even organigramic cases, etc. And I wonder in what measure (and this is a question I'm asking you) is this precedence compatible with the most simple of data perceptions, meaning those on which *Gestalt theory* was based nearly a century ago. In your book, this is generally translated as follows: once a certain number of sound constituents have been isolated and considered as basic elements, these fundamental elements are then placed in relation to the experience of listening to music (following a model which would apply Fechner's law, using the sensation variant as the logarithm$_{of}$ sensory excitation). How is this compatible with Von Ehrenfels' already-dated reflections on the very banal transposition experiment? It's possible that with a musical phrase which is first heard in C major and then, I don't know, in F$\sharp$ minor, there would be no elements of physics shared between the two groups. Nevertheless, both are perceived as being the "same musical phrase," merely transposed in two different keys. How can it be explained that they are heard as being at least analogous if not identical? Instead of using elements (particles or clouds of particles or logical classes, etc.) as starting points, couldn't we imagine the relationships themselves as coming first and not the two extremities of these relationships? Isn't this what would suggest the use of *glissandi* in your own music? Your use of the glissando would almost be in contradiction to what your theory expounds: you would no longer use *elements* as starting points, but rather their relationships, their intervals, and in relation to one of these intervals, we could say that the sound particles would play merely a secondary role as "trail-markers" between the two extreme points of a glissando, while the glissando itself would be the only perceived reality?

IANNIS XENAKIS

Yes, that's a very good question, because it's true that in the musical domain the words "composition" and "composer" mean to put things together; therefore pre-existing things which are already defined in a certain manner.

BERNARD TEYSSÈDRE

That presupposes a priority for analysis over synthesis. In any case, the way in which the "elements" are first introduced seems contradictory to the more structural aspect of the method of presentation itself.

IANNIS XENAKIS

It doesn't necessarily presuppose that, but it presupposes something else. It presupposes a concrete universe where the composer comes and imposes relationships, structures, constructions and architectures. But this is true only to a certain point, because there is a whole area of music as well as of perception which is absolutely unknown. A large part of *Formalized Music* is, in fact, based on this organization of given sound objects, but another part (the last chapter) starts from a sort of global perception. If I say global perception, I mean where there are no molecules (objects which the composer puts together to create more or less evolved organisms) but a magma of possible punctual states (discontinuous pressure values), within which he is capable of coming up with forms following criteria he himself must invent. The last chapter marks another starting point, entirely in opposition to what you just said. If I've been eager to speak here about discontinuous things, it's because when we speak of pressure samples, we're speaking of discontinuous things. Finally, when we speak of music history, either past or present, this is equally the easiest, most direct, and richest approach possible. We are more familiar, more at ease with discontinuous rather than continuous things when dealing with perceptions as well as judgments, but this in no way excludes undefined or undefinable things.

BERNARD TEYSSÈDRE

I was in no way refering to what is undefined. I said that a melody could be transposed in such a manner that no two of its physical elements remain the same; but nevertheless, it can be recognized as the "same melody." The point of view which comes from the consideration of sonic form as a meaningful totality is entirely different from the point of view which starts with sound particles, or clouds of particles before establishing a relationship between these clouds. To say that the contrary is true would imply confounding perception with sensory stimuli.

IANNIS XENAKIS

Fine, I don't see . . .

BERNARD TEYSSÈDRE

Not one of the sensory stimuli would remain the same, and yet they would be perceived in the same manner?

IANNIS XENAKIS

Yes, but be careful. There you are speaking about different levels of perception. When you say the notes aren't the same, all right. There are not only notes though in a melody; there are relationships between the notes—intervals, etc.

BERNARD TEYSSÈDRE

That's precisely what I said: that from a sort of "molecular" point of view, we can oppose a "relational" point of view, according to which these infamous molecules would merely be the extreme points of the relationships.

IANNIS XENAKIS

Naturally! In this book, *Formalized Music*, I'm dealing with relationships between levels (both in the plural), especially with the higher levels, over and above the elements!

BERNARD TEYSSÈDRE

So be it. Let's move on to another question. It has a little bit to do with what was said earlier about the notion of style.

I wonder if in your theoretical and compositional works, priority isn't given to the notion of *saturation*: in other words, a kind of option or subjective taste for dense, full, and not rarefied sonic spaces. It is striking to read on p. 56 of *Formalized Music*: "The ergodic principle states that the capricious effect of an operation that depends on chance is regularized more and more as the operation is repeated." However, it's just possible that the choice itself of the ergodic principle is of a *stylistic* nature. It's possible that it is a subjective option, or one of personal taste, which motivates Xenakis to choose saturated rather than rarefied sonic spaces, to choose large numbers over rare individuals, as Leibnitz would say, those whose definition would imply infinite analysis. It is without a doubt that the will to control prevails over the saturation of sonic spaces out of an economical principle (but this economic principle is also a claim for power). We could very well imagine the inverse option which would distinguish a preference for rare individuals from uncontrollable chance. In summary, John Cage's or Marietan's choice are the polar opposite to Xenakis' choices.

IANNIS XENAKIS

I think you are confusing many things. Excuse me for telling you that. To get back to ergodism: the definition given there is a mathematical one; I was not the one to say it.

BERNARD TEYSSÈDRE

I know that well enough.

IANNIS XENAKIS

I found it in a book by a very important French mathematician who wrote about Markov chains in the forties, Maurice Fréchet. He gives this definition of ergodic processes, of ergodicity. But this is absolutely restricted to this one aspect of my work. On the other hand, when we speak of chance, we must be extremely careful.

BERNARD TEYSSÈDRE

More than the simple fact of using probabilistic calculations as a principle, a repeated choice in favor of large numbers seems to me to imply a preference for control over plentitudes rather than over rare events, which, in themselves, would not be controllable.

IANNIS XENAKIS

But I did a whole study around rare events and rarification in *Achorripis** and other compositions. It's a question of density, and density is a notion which I treat at length and in depth in *Formalized Music.*

*See Catalogue of Works, p. 117.

BERNARD TEYSSÈDRE

Doesn't your music favor *fortissimo* and *pianissimo* for example rather than any impalpable nuances; vast sonic masses rather than voids or silence; an intense emotional charge rather than meditative destitution?

IANNIS XENAKIS

It's true that I haven't written a lot of rarefied music.

BERNARD TEYSSÈDRE

No, not a lot of rarefied music. Nor music which would try to captue individual events, in the way that Olivier Messiaen has used bird song or in the way that John Cage used the fortuitous encounter of seven radios, each broadcasting a different program. In these types of music, there is room for rare encounters instead of finding a relentless search, as there seems to me to be in this book, *Formalized Music*, for highly probable encounters (even if you were to deviate from this later).

IANNIS XENAKIS

It's much more complex than that. First of all, "highly probable" has no meaning except in relation to probability distributions which would be known *a priori*, and concerning certain groups of well-defined events. The notion of fortuity or the unpredictable is fundamental to probability. What is highly probable does not contradict what is highly fortuituous and becomes predictable and is no longer fortuituous not only stochastically, but eventually statistically too. Consequently, whenever an event occurs within a given group, everything happens as if we were in front of a phenomenon created by chance. It occurs unexpectedly and is therefore "rare" in the strictest meaning of periodicity. On the other hand, we can turn on several radios at once, but as soon as they are turned on, we find ourselves in front of a "fait accompli" and therefore a determinacy void of chance. In this case, everything happens as if we were in front of a globally predictable phenomenon even though it is locally fortuituous. This then would constitute the definition of what is highly probable. In some way, the two approaches are equivalent. The appreciable difference is that, in my case, I tried to create not only chains of events but also the events themselves in a manner which would be much more faithful and homogeneous to the basic idea of unpredictability and fortuity. On the other hand, the notion of rarity is relative to an ensemble of possible states and their recurrences. Many or few recurrences of a given event, are decoded in time by the notion of *density* (of rarity). Moreover, the second chapter of *Formalized Music* begins with rare events and their treatment.

BERNARD TEYSSÈDRE
You deal with them in order to dismiss them . . .

IANNIS XENAKIS
No, not at all . . .

BERNARD TEYSSÈDRE
. . . or to relegate them to a secondary order of importance . . .

IANNIS XENAKIS
No, because from the technical point of view, I begin with Poisson's formula which specifically deals with rare events and which I also integrate into my compositions. All this said and done, rare events are rare only in relation to the temporal scale. And there are times when rare events can be considered dense and frequent. In fact, if the chosen temporal unit is small enough, the events within a given music work can seem aggregated in a rarified manner. On the other hand, if the chosen temporal unit is sufficiently large, the same events will seem denser or closer together although they are distributed in the same manner and will create the same fortuitous encounters. Qualitatively speaking therefore, it is the same phenomenon. It's like when you place a Geiger counter close to a radioactive source, or when you move it away: the probability distribution is the same, independent of the distance (the temporal unit). It's the same phenomenon. It's the same law.

BERNARD TEYSSÈDRE
Yes, but will you pardon me if I try to get back to what Michel Serres said earlier when he posed the problem, but I must repeat that we could also conceive of a different type of musician who would not propose to create order from noise but, on the contrary, would strive to isolate the rare, individual events as such; for example, John Cage or Marietan. Not to encourage any one, rare

event to rise out of disorder, but on the contrary, to accept it as an individual event for which an exhaustive analysis would be impossible because infinite.

IANNIS XENAKIS

That's what I'm trying to say.

BERNARD TEYSSÈDRE

But how is it that this Xenakis here, and not another, was able to manage this? Once again, we find ourselves back to the problem of personal style which we already mentioned . . .

IANNIS XENAKIS

Consider rare events within an ensemble of other events, and apply a temporal relationship in order to obtain rarification. Certainly you'll find the rare events isolated. But if you conceive of the ensemble of events globally, the rare events will appear on a background within a much more complex environment. Logically, it would be a question of surrounding a sonic event with rests to the left, to the right; but this is not fundamental. It's a question of scale which corresponds to the degree of attention you pay to this event, therefore, to the degree of prominence you choose to give it and which is a decision based on aesthetic order. But neither in the universe nor in time is there anything unique, "either in nature" or in human thinking. This means that, on the contrary, an event's periodicity (in the broadest sense) and its recurrence unto itself or within its environment is absolutely natural and even unthinkable otherwise.

BERNARD TEYSSÈDRE

Surely, yet a certain restriction of the global field has intervened in your initial choice of elements, which means that the chosen matrix no longer contains even the totality of possibilities but only because it is initially agreed upon that there will be, for example, an orchestra. These preliminary choices no longer let us incorporate some listener's cough or a flying buzzing around the hall into the realm of possible sounds and thereby integrating the fly or the cough as part of the music, as John Cage would. This brings up another musical principle, different than yours.

IANNIS XENAKIS

Fine, and I'll tell you why. Very simply because we all have fortuitous sounds in our daily life. They are completely banal and boring. I'm not interested in reproducing banalities.

BERNARD TEYSSÈDRE

I completely agree with you; what I want to point out is that, in your case, it's a question of aesthetic choice.

OLIVIER REVAULT D'ALLONNES

I believe, nevertheless, that in *Formalized Music*, on page 114, there is an element of a potential answer which tends to agree with what Teyssèdre said. It has to do with musical strategy and *Duel.*[*] On page 113-14 you list the six events which can occur; a cloud of particles, sustained strings, percussions, etc., and silence is the sixth and last event. I'll draw no conclusions for the time being. Then, on pages 114 (in the Table of Evaluations) and p. 115 (in Matrix M2) you mention only five events, the first five, which are the sonic events. Silence has disappeared and doesn't reappear again until the bottom of the page (Matrix M2, p. 115). Why then have you silently (if I may say) passed over this silence only to reinject it in the second table (M2)? You say, "The introduction of the move of silence (VI) modified (M1), and matrix (M2) results." (p. 115). And now, I'm referring to the bottom of page 114 in *Formalized Music* where the different events can be evaluated as "good, good+," etc. and where silence receives a "passing grade" or no grade whatsoever. In summary, you don't like silence.

IANNIS XENAKIS

Silence is banal.

BERNARD TEYSSÈDRE

I don't want to go beyond the scope of this debate. It's clear that M. Revault d'Allonnes does not contest the fecundity of the perspectives opened by Iannis Xenakis. And certainly, neither do I. For my part, what I do fear a bit is that these fertile perspectives could appear imperialistic when seen from the outside. I want to say that a very personal musical theory subtending a very per-

*See Catalogue of Works, p. 117.

sonal musical research could only know how to break down other, different, not to mention opposing musical theories. In the same way, computer programming of serial paintings does not render the most accidental painting obsolete, neither a Michaux "informal" print or a Pollack "action painting." Painting-painting, in the sense of support/surface did not relegate non-painting (in the Dadaist meaning) to the margin. I'd almost say that if metaphysics is an experiment around one idea, as Heidegger claims, then this cluster of doctrines which we have just been discussing constitutes more of a musical metaphysics than a musical science. From this side of his scientism, Iannis Xenakis takes a certain aim at science. The presented *corpus* can be as scientific as we please, but the subjacent goal of this *corpus* is not from the same category as the *corpus* itself, and it's perhaps here that the personal coefficient, this subjective question of style which we have debated, intervenes. It seems to me that choice criteria come into play: choices which subtend this thesis and which, henceforth, this same thesis holds as a certain number of percipients at its secret foundation. I would certainly consider Xenakis' theoretical writings in the same manner as Alberti's treatise, as a sort of "legitimate construction, " "legitimate" provided that it does not become normative and that it accepts other methods of construction to subsist along side and against it, and that these will be considered just as legitimate. Of course, before being able to say that, it would have been necessary to develop other themes. I didn't because of lack of time. Briefly, however, I would have liked to discuss problems concerning the relationship between *in-time* and *outside-time*. This seems to me to throw a certain philosophy of time into question, a conception which would oscillate between the Aristotelian idea of *time as movement's number* on the one hand, and on the other, the notion (different, without a doubt), of *time as an event's fourth dimension*. In no way would this involve unveiling, once again, the old Bergsonian paradox: time *versus* duration. What is in question is time which unravels in a linear, orderly manner; time which belongs to the same system of thought as Leibniz' Monad (unravelling from a mathematical function), or to Hegel's concept of the sphere which is always-already-there from within-itself, unravelling itself for itself in a methodical cycle. This concept of time is that of the western world, that of Mother Greece, where time drew first from one then from the other of its two sides: *logic* and *rhetoric*. According to such a conception, music is thinkable, is thought of as "discourse." To transpose a phrase of Barbaud, who affirmed his being on the look-out for "non-Beethovian music," I would say that, in agreement first with Greek and then with western tradition, Xenakis proposes an *axiom of generalized Beethovian music.* Is this the only possible music? I evoked Barbaud, but couldn't we also evoke the Japanese Gagaku, the all-already-together, the irradiation of the same-around-the-same, all instead of the logico-rhetorical chain which is western musical "discourse," this passage from the same to the same's other? And, going back to my original point, once we see that we could hold our own within the western "discourse," how can we reconcile these two extremes points of its pendular oscillation: sometimes time as an "event's fourth dimension," and sometimes time as "movement's number"? In this second case, movement would come first, and far from being one of the coordinates in series of events, would time merely enumerate the series?

IANNIS XENAKIS

I believe we spoke of that earlier; it's metrics. There is the temporal flow, which is an immediate given, and then there is metrics, which is a construction man makes upon time. And we can't avoid this. Whether you are a musician or a physicist, you have to cross the same bridge. I'll answer you on another point: in no way do I exclude other musical approaches and I really wish you wouldn't accuse me of being an imperialist for what I have done.

BERNARD TEYSSÈDRES

No, no. Xenakis is not at all an imperialist. It is even possible that behind his highly scientific approach. Xenakis remains a profound humanist while he works at his music: he allows a personal style to shine through, the artist's "Me." His choices are well made, and his music is excellent. These choices though, are based on what, (aside from science) if not idiosyncratic choices made by a powerful personality, rich in initiatives? A sub-Xenakis who would apply Xenakis' science, without having Xenakis' personality, could never musically produce more than sub-Xenakis. Don't these choices, so well-made, allow an irrational or unfounded part to subsist? To take an example which clearly illustrates the distance between two personalities, both with great breadth: when Barbaud resorts to the computer, it's the program itself which is the musical work. We can hear a quantity of sonic versions stemming from the same program, without any one of these versions being preferable to another since the work exists on the other side of its audible variants. On the other hand, it seems to me that Xenakis' ear would not judge all of the versions as being equal; he would find a certain number of "preferable" versions, and scores would then preserve those whose sonic effect would have been "preferred." Isn't this (with the exception of the Polytopes) often the case?

IANNIS XENAKIS

But this is my right, my privilege. It's my task to prefer one thing over another.

BERNARD TEYSSÈDRE

Undoubtedly, since this is how your personality is determined. However, your maxim is not at all obvious; even at the risk of repeating myself, Barbaud doesn't have preferences. He composes his program and any result is equal to all the others. Xenakis—and it's his right—has his preferences.

IANNIS XENAKIS

But that's natural. It's absolutely normal.

BERNARD TEYSSÈDRE

Yours will be the last word. The jury will now retire in order to deliberate.

(After a brief deliberation, the jury came back and its Chairman announced that the title of Doctor of Letters and Human Sciences had been **awarded** with "Very Honorable" mention to Iannis Xenakis.)

APPENDIX I

CORRESPONDENCES BETWEEN CERTAIN DEVELOPMENTS IN MUSIC AND MATHEMATICS*

by Iannis Xenakis

MUSIC	MATHEMATICS
500 BC	
Pitches and lengths of strings are being related. Music here gives a marvelous thrust to number theory and geometry. Music invents incomplete scales.	Discovery of the fundamental importance of natural numbers and invention of positive rational numbers (fractions).
No correspondence in music.	Positive irrational numbers, e.g. square root of 2 (Pythagorean theorem).
300 BC	
Invention of the ascending, descending, and null intervals of pitches, in the additive language introduced by Aristoxenos, who also proclaims, in theory, a complete equally-tempered chromatic scale with the twelfth of a tone as the modulus (step). In parallel, there is a continuation of work with the multiplicative (geometric) language of the string lengths which, in fact, is a translation of the additive pitch language (Euclid). Thus, music theory highlights the discovery of the isomorphism between the logarithms (musical intervals) and exponentials (string lengths) more than 15 centuries before their discovery in mathematics; also a premonition of group theory by Aristoxenos.	No reaction in mathematics. Mathematics is left behind in respect to musical theory and practice and it lies dormant in the West, during more than 15 centuries, in spite of the concept of infiniteness and of differential and integral calculus, first sensed by Archimedes.

*Originally appeared in *Musique. Architecture*, (Tornai, 1976) pp. 192-96.

1000 AD

Invention of the two dimensional spatial representation of pitches linked with time by means of staves and points, (represented by Guido d'Arezzo) in advance by three centuries of the coordinates of Oresme and by seven centuries (1635-1637) of the magnificent analytical geometry of Fermat and Descartes.

No parallel in mathematics.

1500 AD

No response or development of the preceding concepts.

Zero and negative numbers are adopted. Construction of the set of rationals.

1600 AD

No equivalence, no reaction.

The sets of real numbers and of logarithms are invented.

1700 AD and 1800 AD

Rediscovery, through practice, of the well-tempered chromatic scale (acme with Johann Sebastian Bach). Music is now left behind in the field of basic structures; but, on the contrary, tonal structures, polyphony, and the invention of macroforms (fugue, sonata) are in advance of and bring to light the seeds that most certainly will inoculate a new life in the music of today and tomorrow. The fugue, for example, is an abstract automaton used two centuries before the birth of the science of automata. Also, unconscious manipulation of finite groups (Klein group) in the four variations of a melodic line used in counterpoint.

Number theory is ahead of, but has no equivalent yet, in temporal structures. These structures will come later with stochastic processes, game theory, automata, etc. Invention of the field of complex numbers (Euler, Gauss). quaternions (Hamilton), definition of continuity (Cauchy), and invention of group structures (Galois, Abel).

1900 AD

Liberation from the tonal yoke. First acceptance of the neutrality of the chromatic totality (Loquin [1895], Hauer, Schoenberg).

Infinite and transinifinte numbers (Cantor). Peano's axiomatics of natural numbers. The beautiful measure theory (Lebesque , Borel, Heine).

1920 AD

First radical formalization of macro-structures through the serial system of Schoenberg.

No new development of number theory. A discussion of some older contradictions in set theory. (Music will catch up in the coming years.)

1930 AD

Reintroduction of finer pitch gradations througth the use of quarter tones, sixth tones, etc., although still plunged in the tonal system. (Wichnegradsky, Haba, Carillo.)

1950 AD

Second radical formalization of macro-structures, with permutations, pitch modes of limited transpositions, and non-retrogradable rhythms (Messiaen).

1953 AD

Introduction of the continuous scale of pitches and time (use of real numbers) by calculating the characteristics of sound, even if, for reasons of perception and interpretation, the real numbers are approximated with rationals. (This is my own contribution, theoretical as well as musical, which also included the use of various domains of mathematics such as probability, logic, calculus, and several structures including group structure. These will play an important role later in macro- and microcomposition.)

1957 AD

New formalizations in music on the macrostructure level: stochastic processes, Markov chains, though used in quite different ways (Hiller, Xenakis), and also the use of computers (Hiller).

1960 AD

Axiomatics of the musical scales with the "sieve theory"* and introduction of complex numbers in composition (this is also a result of my personal work).

1970 AD

New proposals in the microstructure of sounds by the introduction of continuous discontinuity with the aid of probability laws (random walks, Brownian movement). This continuous discontinuity is extended to macrostructures, thus introducing another architectural aspect on a macro- level, for example, in instrumental music (this is also a result of my personal work).

*cf. Appendix II, p, 103.

APPENDIX II

SIEVE THEORY *

It is necessary to give an axiomatization for the totally ordered structure (additive group structure = additive Aristoxenean structure) of the tempered chromatic scale.** The axiomatics of the tempered chromatic scale is based on Peano's axiomatics of numbers:

Preliminary terms. O = the stop at the origin; n = a stop; n' = a stop resulting from elementary displacement of n; D = the set of values of the particular sound characteristic (pitch, density, intensity, instant, speed, disorder . . .). The values are identical with the stops of the displacements.

First propositions (axioms).

1. Stop O is an element of D.

2. If stop n is an element of D then the new stop n' is an element of D.

3. If stops n and m are elements of D then the new stops n' and m' are identical if, and only if, stops n and m are identical.

4. If stop n is an element of D, it will be different from stop O at the origin.

5. If elements belonging to D have a special property P, such that stop O also has it, and if, for every element n of D having this property the element n' has it also, all the elements of D will have the property P.

We have just defined axiomatically a tempered chromatic scale not only of pitch, but also of all the sound properties or characteristics referred to above in D (density, intensity . . .). Moreover, this abstract scale, as Bertrand Russell has rightly observed, à propos the axiomatics of numbers of Peano, has no unitary displacement that is either predetermined or related to an absolute size. Thus it may be constructed with tempered semitones, with Aristoxenean segments (twelfth-tones), with the commas of Didymos (81/80), with quarter-tones, with whole tones, thirds, fourths, fifths, octaves, etc. or with any other unit that is not a factor of a perfect octave.

Now let us define another equivalent scale based on this one but having a unitary displacement which is a multiple of the first. It can be expressed by the concept of *congruence modulo m*.

*Reprinted from *Formalized Music: Thought and Mathematics in Composition*, (Bloomington, Indiana University Press, 1971) with permission of the Publisher.
** Cf. my text on disc L.D.X. A-8368, issued by Le Chant du Monde.
See also *Gravesaner Blätter*, no. 29, and Chap. VI of *Formalized Music*.

Definition. Two integers x and n are said to be *congruent modulo m* when m is a factor of $x - n$. It may be expressed as follows: $x \equiv n \pmod{m}$. Thus, two integers are congruent modulo m when and only when they differ by an exact (positive or negative) multiple of m; e.g., $4 \equiv 19 \pmod 5$, $3 \equiv 13 \pmod 8$, $14 \equiv 0 \pmod 7$.

Consequently, every integer is congruent modulo m with one and with only one value of n:

$$n = (0, 1, 2, \ldots, m - 2, m - 1).$$

Of each of these numbers it is said that it forms a *residual class modulo m*; they are, in fact, the smallest non-negative residues modulo m. $x \equiv n \pmod{m}$ is thus equivalent to $x = n + km$, where k is an integer.

$$k \in Z = \{0, \pm 1, \pm 2, \pm 3, \ldots\}.$$

For a given n and for any $k \in Z$, the numbers x will belong by definition to the residual class n modulo m. This class can be denoted m_n.

In order to grasp these ideas in terms of music, let us take the tempered semitone of our present-day scale as the unit of displacement. To this we shall again apply the above axiomatics, with say a value of 4 semitones (major third) as the elementary displacement.* We shall define a new chromatic scale. If the stop at the origin of the first scale is a $D\sharp$, the second scale will give us all the multiples of 4 semitones, in other words a "scale" of major thirds: $D\sharp$, G, B, $D'\sharp$, G', B'; these are the notes of the first scale whose order numbers are congruent with 0 modulo 4. They all belong to the residual class 0 modulo 4. The residual classes 1, 2, and 3 modulo 4 will use up all the notes of this chromatic total. These classes may be represented in the following manner:

residual class 0 modulo 4: 4_0
residual class 1 modulo 4: 4_1
residual class 2 modulo 4: 4_2
residual class 3 modulo 4: 4_3
residual class 4 modulo 4: 4_0, etc.

Since we are dealing with a sieving of the basic scale (elementary displacement by one semitone), each residual class forms a sieve allowing certain elements of the chromatic continuity to pass through. By extension the chromatic total will be represented as sieve 1_0. The scale of fourths will be given by sieve 5_n, in which $n = 0, 1, 2, 3, 4$. Every change of the index n will entail a transposition of this gamut. Thus the Debussian whole-tone scale, 2_n with $n = 0, 1$, has two transpositions:

---

* Among themselves the elementary displacements are like the integers, that is, they are defined like elements of the same axiomatics.

$$2_0 \to C, D, E, F\sharp, G\sharp, A\sharp, C \cdots$$
$$2_1 \to C\sharp, D\sharp, F, G, A, B, C\sharp \cdots$$

Starting from these elementary sieves we can build more complex scales—all the scales we can imagine—with the help of the three operations of the Logic of Classes: union (disjunction) expressed as $\vee$, intersection (conjunction) expressed as $\wedge$, and complementation (negation) expressed as a bar inscribed over the modulo of the sieve. Thus

$2_0 \vee 2_1$ = chromatic total (also expressible as 1_0)
$2_0 \wedge 2_1$ = no notes, or empty sieve, expressed as $\varnothing$
$\overline{2}_0 = 2_1$ and $\overline{2}_1 = 2_0$.

The major scale can be written as follows:

$$(\overline{3}_2 \wedge 4_0) \vee (\overline{3}_1 \wedge 4_1) \vee (3_2 \wedge 4_2) \vee (\overline{3}_0 \wedge 4_3).$$

By definition, this notation does not distinguish between all the modes on the white keys of the piano, for what we are defining here is the scale; modes are the architectures founded on these scales. Thus the white-key mode D, starting on D, will have the same notation as the C mode. But in order to distinguish the modes it would be possible to introduce non-commutativity in the logical expressions. On the other hand each of the 12 transpositions of this scale will be a combination of the cyclic permutations of the indices of sieves modulo 3 and 4. Thus the major scale transposed a semitone higher (shift to the right) will be written

$$(\overline{3}_0 \wedge 4_1) \vee (\overline{3}_2 \wedge 4_2) \vee (3_0 \wedge 4_3) \vee (\overline{3}_1 \wedge 4_0),$$

and in general

$$(\overline{3}_{n+2} \wedge 4_n) \vee (\overline{3}_{n+1} \wedge 4_{n+1}) \vee (3_{n+2} \wedge 4_{n+2}) \vee (\overline{3}_n \wedge 4_{n+3}),$$

where n can assume any value from 0 to 11, but reduced after the addition of the constant index of each of the sieves (moduli), modulo the corresponding sieve. The scale of D transposed onto C is written

$$(3_n \wedge 4_n) \vee (\overline{3}_{n+1} \wedge 4_{n+1}) \vee (\overline{3}_n \wedge 4_{n+2}) \vee (\overline{3}_{n+2} \wedge 4_{n+3}).$$

Musicology

Now let us change the basic unit (elementary displacement ELD) of the sieves and use the quarter-tone. The major scale will be written

$$(8_n \wedge \overline{3}_{n+1}) \vee (8_{n+2} \wedge \overline{3}_{n+2}) \vee (8_{n+4} \wedge 3_{n+1}) \vee (8_{n+6} \wedge \overline{3}_n),$$

with $n = 0, 1, 2, \ldots, 23$ (modulo 3 or 8). The same scale with still finer sieving (one octave = 72 Aristoxenean segments) will be written

$$(8_n \wedge (9_n \vee 9_{n+6})) \vee (8_{n+2} \wedge (9_{n+3} \vee 9_{n+6})) \vee (8_{n+4} \wedge 9_{n+3})$$
$$\vee (8_{n+6} \wedge (9_n \vee 9_{n+3})),$$

with $n = 0, 1, 2, \ldots, 71$ (modulo 8 or 9).

One of the mixed Byzantine scales, a disjunct system consisting of a chromatic tetrachord and a diatonic tetrachord, second scheme, separated by a major tone, is notated in Aristoxenean segments as 5, 19, 6; 12; 11, 7, 12, and will be transcribed logically as

$$(8_n \wedge (9_n \vee 9_{n+6})) \vee (9_{n+6} \wedge (8_{n+2} \vee 8_{n+4}))$$
$$\vee (8_{n+5} \wedge (9_{n+5} \vee 9_{n+8})) \vee (8_{n+6} \vee 9_{n+3}),$$

with $n = 0, 1, 2, \ldots, 71$ (modulo 8 or 9).

The Raga Bhairavi of the Andara-Sampurna type (pentatonic ascending, heptatonic descending),[*] expressed in terms of an Aristoxenean basic sieve (comprising an octave, periodicity 72), will be written as:
Pentatonic scale:

$$(8_n \wedge (9_n \vee 9_{n+3})) \vee (8_{n+2} \wedge (9_n \vee 9_{n+6})) \vee (8_{n+6} \wedge 9_{n+3})$$

Heptatonic scale:

$$(8_n \wedge (9_n \vee 9_{n+3})) \vee (8_{n+2} \wedge (9_n \vee 9_{n+6})) \vee (8_{n+4} \wedge (9_{n+4} \vee 9_{n+6}))$$
$$\vee (8_{n+6} \wedge (9_{n+3} \vee 9_{n+6}))$$

with $n = 0, 1, 2, \ldots, 71$ (modulo 8 or 9).

These two scales expressed in terms of a sieve having as its elementary displacement, ELD, the comma of Didymos, ELD = 81/80 (81/80 to the power 55.8 = 2), thus having an octave periodicity of 56, will be written as:
Pentatonic scale:

$$(7_n \wedge (8_n \vee 8_{n+6})) \vee (7_{n+2} \wedge (8_{n+5} \vee 8_{n+7})) \vee (7_{n+5} \wedge 8_{n+1})$$

Heptatonic scale:

$$(7_n \wedge (8_n \vee 8_{n+6})) \vee (7_{n+2} \wedge (8_{n+5} \vee 8_{n+7})) \vee (7_{n+3} \wedge 8_{n+3})$$
$$\vee (7_{n+4} \wedge (8_{n+4} \vee 8_{n+6})) \vee (7_{n+5} \wedge 8_{n+1})$$

for $n = 0, 1, 2, \ldots, 55$ (modulo 7 or 8).

We have just seen how the sieve theory allows us to express any scale in terms of logical (hence mechanizable) functions, and thus unify our study of the structures of superior range with that of the total order. It can be useful in entirely new constructions. To this end let us imagine complex,

---

[*] Cf. Alain Daniélou, *Northern Indian Music* (Barnet, Hertfordshire: Halcyon Press, 1954), vol. II, p. 72.

non–octave-forming sieves.* Let us take as our sieve unit a tempered quarter-tone. An octave contains 24 quarter-tones. Thus we have to construct a compound sieve with a periodicity other than 24 or a multiple of 24, thus a periodicity non-congruent with $k \cdot 24$ modulo 24 (for $k = 0, 1, 2, \ldots$). An example would be any logical function of the sieve of moduli 11 and 7 (periodicity $11 \times 7 = 77 \neq k \cdot 24$), $(\overline{11_n \vee 11_{n+1}}) \wedge 7_{n+6}$. This establishes an asymmetric distribution of the steps of the chromatic quarter-tone scale. One can even use a compound sieve which throws periodicity outside the limits of the audible area; for example, any logical function of modules 17 and 18 ($f[17, 18]$), for $17 \times 18 = 306 > (11 \times 24)$.

Suprastructures

One can apply a stricter structure to a compound sieve or simply leave the choice of elements to a stochastic function. We shall obtain a statistical coloration of the chromatic total which has a higher level of complexity.

Using metabolae. We know that at every cyclic combination of the sieve indices (transpositions) and at every change in the module or moduli of the sieve (modulation) we obtain a metabola. As examples of metabolic transformations let us take the smallest residues that are prime to a positive number r. They will form an Abelian (commutative) group when the composition law for these residues is defined as multiplication with reduction to the least positive residue with regard to r. For a numerical example let $r = 18$; the residues 1, 5, 7, 11, 13, 17 are primes to it, and their products after reduction modulo 18 will remain within this group (closure). The finite commutative group they form can be exemplified by the following fragment:

$$5 \times 7 = 35; 35 - 18 = 17;$$
$$11 \times 11 = 121; 121 - (6 \times 18) = 13; \text{etc.}$$

Modules 1, 7, 13 form a cyclic sub-group of order 3. The following is a logical expression of the two sieves having modules 5 and 13:

$$L(5, 13) = (\overline{13_{n+4} \vee 13_{n+5} \vee 13_{n+7} \vee 13_{n+9}})$$
$$\wedge 5_{n+1} \vee (\overline{5_{n+2} \vee 5_{n+4}}) \wedge 13_{n+9} \vee 13_{n+6}.$$

One can imagine a transformation of modules in pairs, starting from the Abelian group defined above. Thus the cinematic diagram (in-time) will be

$$L(5, 13) \to L(11, 17) \to L(7, 11) \to L(5, 1) \to L(5, 5) \to \cdots \to L(5, 13)$$

so as to return to the initial term (closure).**

---

* This perhaps fulfills Edgard Varèse's wish for a spiral scale, that is, a cycle of fifths which would not lead to a perfect octave. This information, unfortunately abridged, was given me by Odile Vivier. (I.X.)

** These last structures were used in *Akrata* (1964) for sixteen winds, and in *Nomos alpha* (1965) for solo cello.

This sieve theory can be put into many kinds of architecture, so as to create included or successively intersecting classes, thus stages of increasing complexity; in other words, orientations towards increased determinisms in selection, and in topological textures of neighborhood.

Subsequently we can put into in-time practice this veritable histology of outside-time music by means of temporal functions, for instance by giving functions of change—of indices, moduli, or unitary displacement—in other words, encased logical functions parametric with time.

Sieve theory is very general and consequently is applicable to any other sound characteristics that may be provided with a totally ordered structure, such as intensity, instants, density, degrees of order, speed, etc. I have already said this elsewhere, as in the axiomatics of sieves. But this method can be applied equally to visual scales and to the optical arts of the future.

Moreover, in the immediate future we shall witness the exploration of this theory and its widespread use with the help of computers, for it is entirely mechanizable. Then, in a subsequent stage, there will be a study of partially ordered structures, such as are to be found in the classification of timbres, for example, by means of lattice or graph techniques.

Conclusion

I believe that music today could surpass itself by research into the outside-time category, which has been atrophied and dominated by the temporal category. Moreover this method can unify the expression of fundamental structures of all Asian, African, and European music. It has a considerable advantage: its mechanization—hence tests and models of all sorts can be fed into computers, which will effect great progress in the musical sciences.

In fact, what we are witnessing is an industrialization of music which has already started, whether we like it or not. It already floods our ears in many public places, shops, radio, TV, and airlines, the world over. It permits a consumption of music on a fantastic scale, never before approached. But this music is of the lowest kind, made from a collection of outdated clichés from the dregs of the musical mind. Now it is not a matter of stopping this invasion, which, after all, increases participation in music, even if only passively. It is rather a question of effecting a qualitative conversion of this music by exercising a radical but constructive critique of our ways of thinking and of making music. Only in this way, as I have tried to show in the present study, will the musician succeed in dominating and transforming this poison that is discharged into our ears, and only if he sets about it without further ado. But one must also envisage, and in the same way, a radical conversion of musical education, from primary studies onwards, throughout the entire world (all national councils for music take note). Non-decimal systems and the logic of classes are already taught in certain countries, so why not their application to a new musical theory, such as is sketched out here?

APPENDIX III

NEW PROPOSALS IN MICROSOUND STRUCTURE

FOURIER SERIES–BASIC IMPORTANCE AND INADEQUACY

The physico-mathematical apparatus of acoustics [1] is plunged into the theories of energy propagation in an elastic medium, in which harmonic analysis is the cornerstone.

The same apparatus finds in the units of electronic circuit design the practical medium where it is realized and checked.

The prodigious development of radio and TV transmissions has expanded the Fourier harmonic analysis to very broad and heterogeneous domains.

Other theories, quite far apart, e.g., servomechanisms and probability, find necessary backing in Fourier series.

In music ancient traditions of scales, as well as those of string and pipe resonances, also lead to circular functions and their linear combinations .[2]

In consequence, any attempt to produce a sound artificially could not be conceived outside the framework of the above physico-mathematical and electronic apparatus, which relies on Fourier series.

Indeed the long route traversed by the *acousmatics* of the Pythagoreans seemed to have found its natural bed. Musical theoreticians did base their theories on Fourier, more or less directly, in order to support the argument about the *natural harmony* of tonality. Moreover, in defining tonality, the 20th-century deprecators of the new musical languages based their arguments on the theory of vibration of elastic bodies and media, that is, in the end, on Fourier analysis. But they were thus creating a paradox, for although they wanted to keep music in the intuitive and instinctive domain, in order to legitimize the tonal universe they made use of physico-mathematical arguments!

[1] Stevens, S. S., and Davis, H. *Hearing*. New York: John Wiley and Sons, 1948; Beranek, Leo L. *Acoustics*. New York: McGraw-Hill, 1954.

[2] Appelman, D. Ralph. *The Science of Vocal Pedagogy*. Bloomington: Indiana University Press, 1967.

*Reprinted from *Formalized Music: Thought and Mathematics in Composition*, (Bloomington, Indiana University Press, 1971) with permission of the Publisher.

MICROSOUND STRUCTURES

The Impasse of Harmonic Analysis and Some Reasons

Two major difficulties compel us to think in another way:

1. The defeat by the thrust of the new languages of the theory according to which harmony, counterpoint, etc., must stem, just from the *basis* formed by circular functions. E.g., how can we justify such harmonic configurations of recent instrumental or electro-acoustic music as a cloud of gliding sounds? Thus, harmonic analysis has been short-circuited in spite of touching attempts like Hindemith's explanation of Schönberg's system.[3] Life and sound adventures jostle the traditional theses, which are nevertheless still being taught in the conservatories (rudimentally, of course). It is therefore natural to think that the disruptions in music in the last 60 years tend to prove once again that music and its "rules" are socio-cultural and historical *conditionings*, and hence modifiable. These conditions seem to be based roughly on *a.* the absolute limits of our senses and their deforming power (e.g., Fletcher contours); *b.* our canvass of mental structures, some of which were treated in the preceding chapters (ordering, groups, etc.); *c.* the means of sound production (orchestral instruments, electro-acoustic sound synthesis, storage and transformation analogue systems, digital sound synthesis with computers and digital to analogue converters). If we modify any one of these three points, our socio-cultural conditioning will also tend to change in spite of an obvious inertia inherent in a sort of "entropy" of the social facts.

2. The obvious failure, since the birth of oscillating circuits in electronics, to reconstitute any sound, even the simple sounds of some orchestral instruments! *a.* The Trautoniums, Theremins, and Martenots, all pre-World War II attempts, prove it. *b.* Since the war, all "electronic" music has also failed, in spite of the big hopes of the fifties, to pull electro-acoustic music out of its cradle of the so-called electronic pure sounds produced by frequency generators. Any electronic music based on such sounds only, is marked by their simplistic sonority, which resembles radio atmospherics or heterodyning. The serial system, which has been used so much by electronic music composers, could not by any means improve the result, since it itself is much too elementary. Only when the "pure" electronic sounds were framed by other "concrete" sounds, which were much richer and much more interesting (thanks to E. Varèse, Pierre Schaeffer, and Pierre Henry), could electronic music become really powerful. *c.* The most recent attempts to use the flower of modern technology, computers coupled to converters, have shown that in spite of some relative successes,[4] the sonorous results are even less interesting than those made ten years ago in the classic electro-acoustic studios by means of frequency generators, filters, modulators, and reverberation units.

3 Hindemith, Paul. *The Craft of Musical Composition.* 2 vols. New York: Associated Music Publishers, 1942.
4 Risset, Jean Claude. "An Introductory Catalogue of Computer Synthesized Sounds." Unpublished. Murray Hill, New Jersey: Bell Telephone Laboratories, 1969.

In line with these critiques, what are the causes of these failures? In my opinion the following are some of them:

1. Meyer-Eppler's studies[5] have shown that the spectral analysis of even the simplest orchestral sounds (they will form a reference system for a long time to come) presents variations of spectral lines in frequency as well as in amplitude. But these tiny (second order) variations are among those that make the difference between a lifeless sound made up of a sum of harmonics produced by a frequency generator and a sound of the same sum of harmonics played on an orchestral instrument. These tiny variations, which take place in the permanent, stationary part of a sound, would certainly require new theories of approach, using another functional basis and a harmonic analysis on a higher level, e.g., stochastic processes, Markov chains, correlated or autocorrelated relations, or theses of pattern and form recognition. Even so, analysis theories of orchestral sounds[6] would result in very long and complex calculations, so that if we had to simulate such an orchestral sound from a computer and from harmonic analysis on a first level, we would need a tremendous amount of computer time, which is impossible for the moment.

2. It seems that the transient part of the sound is far more important than the permanent part in timbre recognition and in music in general.[7] Now, the more the music moves toward complex sonorities close to "noise," the more numerous and complicated the transients become, and the more their synthesis from trigonometric functions becomes a mountain of difficulties, even more unacceptable to a computer than the permanent states. It is as though we wanted to express a sinuous mountain silhouette by using portions of circles. In fact, it is thousands of times more complicated. The intelligent ear is infinitely demanding, and its voracity for information is far from having been satisfied. This problem of a considerable amount of calculation is comparable to the 19th-century classical mechanics problem that led to the kinetic gas theory.

3. There is no pattern and form recognition theory, dependent on harmonic analysis or not, that would enable us to translate curves synthesized by means of trigonometric functions in the perception of forms or configurations. For instance, it is impossible for us to define equivalence classes of very diversified oscilloscope curves, which the ear throws into the same bag. Furthermore, the ear makes no distinction between things that actual acoustic theories differentiate (e.g., phase differences, differential sensitivity ability), and vice versa.

---

[5] Meyer-Epler, W. *Grundlagen und Anwendungen der Informations Theorie.* Berlin: Springer-Verlag, 1959.

[6] Von Foerster, Heinz, and Beauchamp, James W., eds. *Music by Computers.* New York: John Wiley and Sons, 1969.

[7] Schaeffer, Pierre. *Traité des objets musicaux: Essai interdisciplines.* Paris: Editions du Seuil, 1966.

The Wrong Concept of Juxtaposing Finite Elements

Perhaps the ultimate reason for such difficulties lies in the improvised entanglement of notions of finity and infinity. For example, in sinusoidal oscillation there is a unit element, the variation included in 2π. Then this *finite* variation is repeated endlessly. Seen as an economy of means, this procedure can be one of the possible optimizations. We labor during a limited span of time (one period), then repeat the product indefinitely with almost no additional labor. Basically, therefore, we have a mechanism (e.g., the sine function) engendering a finite temporal object, which is repeated for as long as we wish. This long object is now considered as a new element, to which we juxtapose similar ones. The odds are that one can draw any variation of one variable (e.g., atmospheric pressure) as a function of time by means of a finite superposition (sum) of the preceding elements. In doing this we expect to obtain an irregular curve, with increasing irregularity as we approach "noises." On the oscilloscope such a curve would look quite complex. If we ask the eye to recognize particular forms or symmetries on this curve it would almost certainly be unable to make any judgment from samples lasting say 10 microseconds because it would have to follow them too fast or too slowly: too fast for the everyday limits of visual attention, and too slow for the TV limits, which plunge the instantaneous judgment into the level of global perception of forms and colors. On the other hand, for the same sample duration, the ear is made to recognize forms and patterns, and therefore senses the correlations between fragments of the pressure curve at various levels of understanding. We ignore the laws and rules of this ability of the ear in the more complex and general cases that we are interested in. However, in the case in which we superpose sine curves, we know that below a certain degree of complexity the ear disentangles the constituents, and that above it the sensation is transformed into timbre, color, power, movement, roughness, and degree of disorder; and this brings us into a tunnel of ignorance. To summarize, we expect that by judiciously piling up simple elements (pure sounds, sine functions) we will create any desired sounds (pressure curve), even those that come close to very strong irregularities—almost stochastic ones. This same statement holds even when the unit element of the iteration is taken from a function other than the sine. In general, and regardless of the specific function of the unit element, this procedure can be called *synthesis by finite juxtaposed elements*. In my opinion it is from here that the deep contradictions stem that should prevent us from using it.*

---

* In spite of this criticism I would like to draw attention to the magnificent manipulatory language Music V of Max V. Mathews, which achieves the final step in this procedure and automates it .[8] This language certainly represents the realization of the dream of an electronic music composer in the fifties.

[8] Mathews, Max V. *The Technology of Computer Music.* Cambridge: M.I.T. Press, 1969.

NEW PROPOSAL IN MICROCOMPOSITION BASED ON PROBABILITY DISTRIBUTIONS

We shall raise the contradiction, and by doing so we hope to open a new path in microsound synthesis research—one that without pretending to be able to simulate already known sounds, will nevertheless launch music, its psychophysiology, and acoustics in a direction that is quite interesting and unexpected.

Instead of starting from the unit element concept and its tireless iteration and from the increasing irregular superposition of such iterated unit elements, we can start from a disorder concept and then introduce means that would increase or reduce it. This is like saying that we take the inverse road: We do not wish to construct a complex sound edifice by using discontinuous unit elements (bricks = sine or other functions); we wish to construct sounds with continuous variations that are not made out of unit elements. This method would use stochastic variations of the sound pressure directly. We can imagine the pressure variations produced by a particle capriciously moving around equilibrium positions along the pressure ordinate in a non-deterministic way. Therefore we can imagine the use of any "random walk" or multiple combinations of them.

Method 1. Every probability function is a particular stochastic variation, which has its own personality (personal behavior of the particle). We shall then use *any* one of them. They can be discontinuous or continuous; e.g., Poisson, exponential (ce^{-cx}), normal, uniform, Cauchy $(t[\pi(t^2+x^2)]^{-1})$, arc sin $(\pi^{-1}[x(1-x)]^{-1/2})$, logistic $[(\alpha e^{-\alpha x-\beta})(1+e^{-\alpha x-\beta})^{-1}]$ distributions.

Method 2. Combinations of a random variable X with itself can be established. Example: If $f(x)$ is the probability function of X we can form $S_n = X_1 + X_2 + \cdots + X_n$ (by means of the n-fold convolution of $f(x)$ with itself) or $P_K = X_1 \cdot X_2 \cdots X_K$, or any linear, polynomial, ..., function of the variable X.

Method 3. The random variables (pressure, time) can be functions of other variables (elastic forces), even of random variables. Example: The pressure variable x is under the influence of a centrifugal or centripetal force $\phi(x, t)$. For instance, if the particle (pressure) is influenced by a force wx (w being a constant) and also obeys a Wiener-Lévy process, then its density will be

$$q_t(x, y) = (w^{1/2}/[\pi(1 - e^{-2wt})]^{-1/2}) \exp[-w(y - xe^{-wt})^2/(1 - e^{-2wt})],$$

where x and y are the values of the variable at the instants 0 and t, respectively. (This is also known as the Ornstein-Uhlenbeck process.)

Method 4. The random variable moves between two reflecting (elastic) barriers. Example: If we again have a Wiener-Lévy process with two reflecting barriers at $a > 0$ and zero, then the density of this random walk will be

113

$$q_t(x, y) = (2\pi t)^{-1/2} \sum_{k=0}^{\pm \infty} (\exp[-(y - x + 2ka)^2/2t]$$
$$+ \exp[-(y + x + 2ka)^2/2t]),$$

where x and y are the values of the variables at the instants 0 and t, respectively, and $k = 0, \pm 1, \pm 2, \ldots$.

Method 5. The parameters of a probability function can be considered as variables of other probability functions (randomization, mixtures).[9]

Examples:

a. t is the parameter of a Poisson distribution $f(k) = (\alpha t)^k (k!)^{-1} e^{-\alpha t}$, and the random variable of the exponential density $g(t) = \beta e^{-\beta t}$. The combination is

$$f(k) * g(t) = w(k) = \int_{-\infty}^{\infty} (\alpha t)^k (k!)^{-1} e^{-\alpha t} \beta e^{-\beta t} \, dt = \beta(\alpha + \beta)^{-1} [\alpha(\alpha + \beta)^{-1}]^k,$$

which is a geometric distribution.

b. p and q are the probabilities of a random walk with jumps ± 1 (Bernoulli distribution). The time intervals between successive jumps are random variables with common density e^{-t} (Poisson distribution). Then the probability of the position n at instant t will be $f_n(t) = I_n(2t\sqrt{pq})e^{-t}(p/q)^{n/2}$, where

$$I_n(x) = \sum_{k=0}^{\infty} [k! \Gamma(k + n + 1)]^{-1} (x/2)^{2k+n}$$

is the modified Bessel function of the first kind of order n.

Method 6. Linear, polynomial, ..., combinations of probability functions f_i are considered as well as composite functions (mixtures of a family of distributions, transformations in Banach space, subordination, etc.).

a. If A and B are any pair of intervals on the line, and $Q(A, B) = \text{prob}\{X \in A, Y \in B\}$ with $q(x, B) = \text{prob}\{X = x, Y \in B\}$ (q, under appropriate regularity conditions being a probability distribution in B for a given x and a continuous function in x for a fixed B; that is, a conditional probability of the event $\{Y \in B\}$, given that $X = x$), and $\mu\{A\}$ is a probability distribution of $x \in A$, then $Q(A, B) = \int_A q(x, B)\mu\{dx\}$ represents a mixture of the family of distributions $q(X, B)$, which depends on the parameter x, with μ serving as the distribution of the randomized parameter [30].

b. Interlocking probability distributions (modulation). If $f_1, f_2, \ldots,$ f_n are the probability distributions of the random variables $X^1, X^2, \ldots,$ X^n, respectively, then we can form

[9] Feller, William. *An Introduction to Probability Theory and Its Applications*. 2 vols. New York: John Wiley and Sons, 1966.

$$S_{\sigma i}^i = X_1^i + X_2^i + \cdots + X_{\sigma i}^i \quad \text{and} \quad S^n\left(\sum_{i=1}^n S_{\sigma i}^i\right) = S_{\sigma 1}^1 + S_{\sigma 2}^2 + \cdots + S_{\sigma n}^n$$

or

$$P_{\gamma k}^k = X_1^k \cdot X_2^k \cdots X_{\gamma k}^k \quad \text{and} \quad P^n\left(\prod_{k=1}^n P_{\gamma k}^k\right) = P_{\gamma 1}^1 \cdot P_{\gamma 2}^2 \cdots P_{\gamma n}^n,$$

or any combination (functional or stochastic) of these sums and products. Furthermore, the σi and γk could be generated by either independent determined functions, independent stochastic processes, or interrelated determined or indetermined processes. In some of these cases we would have the theory of renewal processes, if, for instance, the σi were considered waiting times Ti. From another point of view, some of these cases would also correspond to the time series analysis of statistics. In reality, the ear seems to realize such an analysis when in a given sound it recognizes the fundamental tone pitch together with timbre, fluctuation, or casual irregularities of that sound! In fact, time series analysis should have been invented by composers, if they had—.

c. Subordination [30]. Suppose $\{X(t)\}$, a Markovian process with continuous transition probabilities

$$Q_t(x, \Gamma) = \text{prob}\, \{X(T(t + s)) \in \Gamma | X(T(s)) = x\}$$

(stochastic kernel independent of s), and $\{T(t)\}$, a process with non-negative independent increments. Then $\{X(T(t))\}$ is a Markov process with transition probabilities

$$P_t(x, \Gamma) = \int_0^\infty Q_s(x, \Gamma) U_t\{ds\},$$

where U_t is the infinitely divisible distribution of $T(t)$. This P_t is said to be *subordinated* to $\{X(t)\}$, using the operational time $T(t)$ as the *directing* process.

Method 7. The probability functions can be filed into classes, that is, into parent curve configurations. These classes are then considered as elements of higher order sets. The classification is obtained through at least three kinds of criteria, which can be interrelated: *a.* analytical source of derived probability distribution; gamma, beta, . . ., and related densities, such as the density of χ^2 with n degrees of freedom (Pearson); Student's t density; Maxwell's density; *b.* other mathematical criteria, such as stability, infinite divisibility; and *c.* characteristic features of the curve designs: at level 0, where the values of the random variable are accepted as such; at level 1, where their values are accumulated, etc.

APPENDIX IV

A CATALOGUE OF
MUSICAL WORKS BY IANNIS XENAKIS

(All works published by Editions Salabert, Paris, unless otherwise stated. All works marked with an asterisk (*) are recorded.

String Orchestra/Ensemble

Syrmos (1959)*
> for 18 or 36 strings (6.6.0.4.2.) or doubled.
>> Duration: 14'

Analogiques A and B (1959)*
> for 9 strings (3.3.0.2.1.) and 4-track tape.
>> Duration: 7'

Aroura (1971)*
> for 12 strings (4.3.2.2.1.) or multiple.
>> Duration: 12'

Retours-Windungen (1976)*
> for 12 violoncelli.
>> Duration: 8'

Pour Les Baleines (1982)
> for large string orchestra.
>> Duration: 2'30"

Shaar (1983)
> for large string orchestra.
>> Duration: 14'

Orchestral Music

Metastasis (1953-54)*

for 61 instruments: picc, fl, 2 ob, bass cl, 3 Fr. hn, 2 tpt, 2 tenor tbn, timp, perc (xylo, trgl, wdblk, drums, snare, bass drum, timp) and strings (12.12.8.8.6.).

Duration: 7′

Published by Boosey & Hawkes.

Pithoprakta (1955-56)*

for 50 instruments: 2 tenor tbn, xylophone, woodblock, and strings (12.12.8.8.6.).

Duration: 9′

Published by Boosey & Hawkes.

Duel (1959)

a "game" for 2 orchestras: 2 picc, 2 ob, 2 B-flat cl, 2 E-flat cl, 2 bass cl, 2 bn, 2 cb, 4 tpt, 2 tbn, perc (2 snares, 2 drums, 4 bongos, 6 congas) and strings (2.2.0.8.4.).

Varying duration: around 10′

ST/48 (1962)

for 48 musicians: picc, fl, 2 ob, cl, bass cl, bn, cbn, 2 Fr. hn, 2 tpt, 2 tbn, 4 timp, perc (4 tams, 5 temple blks, drum, vibr, mar) and strings (8.8.6.6.4.).

Duration: 11′

Published by Boosey & Hawkes.

Stratégie (1962)*

a "game" for 2 orchestras: 2 picc, 2 fl, 2 ob, 2 B-flat cl, 2 E-flat cl, 2 bass cl, 2 bn, 2 cbn, 4 Fr. hn, 4 tpt, 4 tenor tbn, 2 tb, perc (2 vibr, 2 mar, 2 maracas, 2 susp. cym, 2 bass drums, 2x4 toms, 2x5 temple-blk, 2x4 wdblk, 2x5 goat bells and strings (12.12.8.8.6.).

Variable duration: between 10′ and 15′

Published by Boosey & Hawkes.

Terretektorh (1965-66)*

for 88 musicians scattered throughout the public: picc, 2 fl, 3 ob, B-flat cl, E-flat cl, bass cl, 2 bn, 3 cbn, 4 Fr. hn, 4 Fr. hn, 4 tpt, 4 tenor tbn, tb, perc and strings (16.14.12.10.8.). Each musician must also have in his/her possession: 1 wdblk, 1 whip, 1 maracus, 1 Acme siren.

Duration: 18′

Polytope De Montreal (1967)*

Sound and light show, with music for 4 identical orchestras: picc, cl, bass cl, cbn, tpt, tenor tbn, perc (lrg. gong, Japanese wdblk, 4 toms) and multiples of 4 vln and 4 vc.

Duration: 6'

Published by Boosey & Hawkes.

Nomos Gamma (1967-68)*

for 98 musicians scattered throughout the public: picc, 2 fl, 3 ob, B-flat cl, E-flat cl, cb cl, 2 bn, 3 cbn, 6 Fr. hn, 5 tpt, 4 tenor tbn, tb, perc (7 players; each having 4 scaled toms plus one timpanist) and strings (16.14.12.10.8.).

Duration: 15'

Kraanerg (1968-69)*

music ballet for 4 track tape and orchestra: picc, ob, 2 tpt, 2 tbn and strings (multiples of 3.3.2.2.2.).

Duration: 75'

Published by Boosey & Hawkes.

Antikhthon (1971)*

ballet music for orchestra: 3.3.3.2.(+ cbn); 4.3.3.1.; perc, strings (10.8.6.6.4).

Duration: 23'

Eridanos (1973)

for 2 Fr. hn, 2 tpt, 2 tb and strings (16.14.12.10.8.).

Duration: 11'

Noomena (1974)

for 3 (+ picc), 3 (+Eng. hn), 3 (+ E-flat cl & bass cl), 3 (+ cbn); 6.5.4.1.; strings (18.16.14.12.10.).

Duration: 17'

Empreintes (1975)

for 1 picc, 2 fl, 2 fl, 3 ob, 1 Eng. hn, 1 E-flat, 2 B-flat cl, 1 bass cl, 2 bn, 1 cbn, 4 Fr. hn, 4 tpt, 4 tenor, tbn, 1 tb, strings (16.14.12.10.8.).

Duration: 12'

Jonchaies (1977)*

for 2 picc, 2 fl, 4 ob, 2 Eng. hn, 1 E-flat cl, 2 B-flat cl, 2 bn, 2

cbn, 6 Fr. hn, 4 tpt, 2 tenor tbn, 2 bass tbn, 1 cb tb, timp, 4 perc (4 sets of 4 toms, 10 Chinese blks, 3 susp cym, bass drum, vibr, xylomarimba) and strings (18.16.14.12.10.).
Durations: 17′

Lichens I (1984)

for 4 fl (1 picc), 4 ob, (1 Eng. hn), 4 B-flat cl, 3 bn (1 cbn), 4 hn in F, 4 tpt, 4 tenor tbn, 2 cb tbn, 1 cb tb, 4 pedal timp, 4 perc: 3x (1 pair bangos, 3 tom-toms, 1 very lrg bass drum), 1 xylo, 1 whip, 1 wdblk, 1 susp cym, 1 lrg Chinese gong, 1 pno and strings (16.14.12.10.8.).
Duration: 16′

Piano and Orchestra

Synaphaï (1969)*

for piano and orchestra: 3.3.3.3; 4.4.4.1; perc (3 unpitched drums); strings (16.14.10.10.8.).
Duration: 14′

Erikhthon (1974)

for piano and orchestra: 3 (+ picc).3.3.(+ bass cl).3 (+ cbn); 4.4.4.1.; strings (16.14.12.10.8.).
Duration: 15′

Baritone, Percussion and Orchestra

Ais (1980)

for Baritone, percussion solo and orchestra: 4. (+ picc).4. (1 Eng. hn).4. (1 bass cl). 4.(1 cbn); 4.4.4.4; perc, pno, strings (16.14.12.10.8.).
Duration: 17′

Chorus and Orchestra

Polla Ta Dhina (1962)*

for children's choir and orchestra: 20 children's voices, picc, fl, 2 ob, cl, bass cl, bn, cbn, 2 Fr. hn, 2 tpt, 2 tbn, perc (vibr, 4 toms, 5 temple-blk, maracas, susp cym, timp) and strings (8.8.6.6.4.).
Duration: 6′
Published by Modern Wewerke Editions.

Cendrées (1973)*

for mixed chorus (36 to 72 voices) and orchestra: 2 (picc). 2.2.(cbn).2; 2.2.2.1; strings (16.14.12.10.8.).
Duration: 25'

Anemoessa (1979)

for chorus and orchestra: 4 fl (1 picc), 4 ob, 4 B-flat cl, 3 bn, 1 cbn, 4 Fr. hn, 4 tpt, 4 tbn, 1 tb, 2 timp, 1 snare; mixed chorus: S.A.T.B. (56 to 80 voices) and strings (16.14.12.10.8.).
Duration: 15'

Nekuia (1981)

for mixed chorus and orchestra: 4 (1 picc).4.4.4; 6.4.4.1; 4 perc, 2 hp, pno and strings (14.12.10.8.8.).
Duration: approx. 26'

Chorus and Ensemble

Oresteia (1965-66)*

stage music for mixed chorus, children's choir and orchestra: picc, ob, cl, bass cl, cbn, Fr. hn, tpt, picc tpt in D-flat, tenor tbn, tb, perc (traditional & unusual instruments)
and vc.
Duration: 100'
Published by Boosey & Hawkes.

Medea (1977)*

stage music for male chorus (also playing rhythms with river or sea stones) and instrumental ensemble: cl, cbn, tpt, vc, perc (4 toms, 3 wdblk, claves, maracas).
Duration: 25'

A Colone (1977)

for male chorus (or women's chorus): 20+ voices, 5 Fr. hn, 3 tbn, 6 vc, 4 db.
Duration: 14'

Pour la Paix (1982)

for mixed chorus, tape and narrators.
Duration: 26'45" cf. also for a capella choir.

Chant des Soleils (1983)

> for mixed chorus, children's choirs, brass (6.6.6.0.) and perc.
> Duration: 8'

Ensemble Music

Achorripsis (1956-57)*

> for 21 instruments: picc, ob, E-flat cl, bass cl, bn, cbn, 2 tpt, tenor tpt, xylo, wdblk, bass drum, 3 vln, 3 vc, 3 db.
> Duration: 7'
> Published by Bote und Bock Editions.

ST/10 (1962)*

> for 10 instruments: cl, bass cl, 2 Fr. hn, hp, perc (5 temple-blk, 4 tom, 2 congas, wdblk) and string quartet.
> Duration: 11'
> Published by Boosey & Hawkes.

Atrees (1960)*

> for 10 instruments: fl, cl, bass cl, Fr. hn, tpt, tbn, perc (maracas, susp cym, gong, 5 temple-blk, 4 toms, vibr), vln, vc.
> Duration: 15'

Eonta (1963)*

> for piano, 2 trumpets and 3 trombones.
> Duration: 18'
> Published by Boosey & Hawkes.

Hiketides (1964)

> instrumental suite for 2 trumpets, 2 trombones, and strings (6.6.0.8.4. or mutiples).
> Duration: 10'

Akrata (1964-65)*

> for 16 wind instruments: picc, ob, B-flat cl, E-flat cl, bass cl,, bn, 2 cbn, 2 Fr. hn, 3 tpt, 2 tenor tbn, tb.
> Duration: 11
> Published by Boosey & Hawkes.

Anaktoria (1969)*
> for cl, bn, hn, 2 vln, vla, vc, db.
>> Duration: 11'

Phlegra (1975)
> for 11 instrumentalists: fl(picc), ob, B-flat cl, bass cl, bn, Fr. hn, tpt, tbn, vln, vla, vc, db.
>> Duration: 14'

N'Shima (1975)
> for 2 Fr. hn, 2 tbn, 2 mezzo-sop, vc.
>> Duration: 17'

Epeï (1976)
> for Eng. hn, B-flat cl, C tpt, 2 tenor tbn, db.
>> Duration: 13'

Akanthos (1977)
> for fl, cl, sop, 2 vlns, vla, vlc, dbl bass, pno.
>> Duration: 11'

Palimpsest (1979)
> for ob, Eng. hn, B-flat cl, bass cl, bn, Fr. hn, pno, perc (2 bongos, 1 tumba, 3 tom-toms, 1 timp) and string quintet.
>> Duration: 11'

Khal Perr (1983)
> for brass quintet and perc: 2 C tpt (2 sopr tpt in B-flat), 1 Fr. hn in F, 1 tbn, 1 tb, 1 perc (vibr, 2 bongos, 3 tom-toms, 1 lrg bass drum).
>> Duration: 10'30"

Analogues A & B (1959)*
> see **String Orchestra/Ensemble**

Aroura (1971)*
> see **String Orchestra/Ensemble**

Retours-Windungen (1976)*
> see **String Orchestra/Ensemble**

A Cappella Chorus

Nuits (1967)*
> for 12 mixed solo voices
>> Duration: 12'

A Helene (1977) text by Euripides for women's chorus
> Duration: 12'

Serment-Orkos (1981) text by Hippocrates for mixed chorus
> Duration: 7'

Pour la Paix (1982)
> version for mixed chorus

Vocal Music

N'Shima (1977)
> see **Ensemble Music**

Akanthos (1975)
> see **Ensemble Music**

Pour Maurice (1982)
> for Baritone and piano.
>> Duration: 4'

Electro-Acoustic Music

Diamorphoses (1957)*
> electro-acoustic music for 4-track tape.
>> Duration: 7' R.T.F.

Concret PH (1958)*
> electro-acoustic music for 4-track tape.
>> Duration: 2'45" R.T.F.

Orient-Occident (1960)*
> electro-acoustic music for 4-track tape.
>> Duration: 12′ R.T.F.

Bohor (1962)*
> electro-acoustic music for 8-track tape (also avail. on 4-track).
>> Duration: 23′

Hibiki Hana Ma (1969-70)*
> electro-acoustic on 12-track tape (also avail. on 4-track) for an audiovisiual show with an orchestral basis.
>> Duration: 18′

Persepolis (1971)*
> light and sound show with electro-acoustic music on 8-track tape (avail. 4-track).
>> Duration: 57′

Polytope de Cluny (1972)
> light and sound show with 7-track tape (avail. on 4-track).
>> Duration: 24′

La Legende D'Eer (1977)
> for the Diatope, light and sound show action for 1600 electronic flashes, 4 lazer beams, 400 mirrors, various optical devices and 7-track tape.
>> Duration: 46′

Mycenes A (1978)
> stereo tape of music composed on the UPIC "musical drawing board" at CEMANu.
>> Duration: 10′

Pour la Paix (1982)
> see **Chorus and Ensemble**

Instrumental Music for Soloists

Piano
Herma (1960-61)*
>> Duration: 9′
>> Published by Boosey & Hawkes.

Evryali (1973)*
    Duration: 11'

Mists (1981)
    Duration: 12'
  Also see:
Morima-Amorsima, String Trios
Eonta, Akanthos, Palimpsest,Ensemble Music
Synaphai, Erikhton, Piano and Orchestra
Dikhthas, Violin and Piano
Pour Maurice, Vocal Music

Harpsichord
Khoaï (1976)*
    Duration: 15'

Naama (1984)
    Duration: 16'

Harpsichord and Percussion
Komboi (1981)*
    Duration: 17'
Organ
Gmeeoorah (1974)
   "Version for 56 note organ"
   "Version for 61 note organ"
    Duration: 29'

Violin
Mikka (1971)*
    Duration: 4'

Mikka "S" (1976)*
    Duration: 5'

Violin and Piano
Dikhthas (1979)*
    Duration: 12'

Viola
Embellie (1981)*
    Duration: around 7'

Violoncello
Nomos Alpha (1966)*
      Duration: 17'
      Published by Boosey & Hawkes.

Kottos (1977)*
      Duration: 11'

Charisma*
see below

Double Bass
Theraps (1975-76)
      Duration: 11'

Oboe and Percussion
Dmaathen (1976)
      Duration: 10'

Clarinet and Violoncello
Charisma (Hommage to Jean-Pirre Guezec: 1971)*
      Duration: 4'

Brass
Eonta (1963-64)*
    for piano and 5 brass: 2 tpt, 3 tenor tbn.
      Duration: 18'
      Published by Boosey & Hawkes.

Linaia-Agon (1972)
    a musical game for tenor, tpt, F tpt, tb.
      Varying duration
      New definite version: 1982

Khal Perr (1983)
    for brass quintet and percussion.

see **Ensemble Music**
Percussion

Psappha (1975)*
      Duration: 13'

Persephassa (1969)*
  for 6 percussionists
    Duration: 24'

Pleiades (1978)
  for 6 percussionists
    Duration: 46'

Also see
Komboi, Harpsichord and Percussion
Dmaathen, Oboe ansd Percussion
Ais, Baritone, Percussion and Orchestra
Khal Perr, Ensemble Music

String Trios
Morsima-Amorsima (1962)*
  for piano, violin, viola, violoncello and double bass.
    Duration: 11
    Published by Boosey & Hawkes.

Ikhoor (1978)*
    Duration: 11'

String Quartets
St/4 (1956-62)*
    Duration: 11'
    Published by Boosey & Hawkes.

Tetras (1983)
    Duration: 16'

BOOKS WRITTEN BY XENAKIS

Musiques Formelles 232 pages. *La Revue Musicale,* special
  double edition 253-54.
  Richard Masse, Paris 1963 (out of print)
  Stock, Paris 1981 (new edition)
  Spirali, Milan 1982 (Italian edition)

Musique Architechture
160 pages. Mutations-Orientation Collection.
Casterman, Tournai 1971 (second edition, revised and enlarged, 238 pages, 1976)
Zen-on Music Co., Tokyo 1976 (Japanese edition, translation by Yuji Takahashi)
Spirali, Milan 1972 (Italian edition)
Antoni Bosch, Barcelona 1982 (Catalan edition)

Formalized Music
273 pages (in English). Indiana University Press, Bloomington, London, 1971
Spirali, Milan 1982 (Italian edition)

BOOKS WRITTEN ABOUT XENAKIS

Iannis Xenakis
L'Arc 51, Paris 1972
Regards sur Iannis Xenakis
Stock, Paris 1981 (articles by 47 authors)
Iannis Xenakis
by N. Matossian. Fayard, Paris 1981
Kahn & Averill, London 1984 (English edition)
Interviews with Iannis Xenakis
by Bálint András Varga, Budapest 1982 (in Hungarian)

APPENDIX V

BIBLIOGRAPHY

MEYER-EPLER, W., *Grundlagen und Anwendungen der Informations Theorie,* Berlin, Springer-Verlag, 1959.

STEVENS, S. S. and DAVIS, H., *Hearing,* New York, John Wiley and sons, 1948.

BERANEK, Leo L., *Acoustics,* New York, Mc Graw-Hill, 1954.

APPELMAN, D. Ralph, *The Science of Vocal Pedagogy,* Bloomington, Indiana University Press, 1967.

HINDEMITH, Paul, *The Craft of Musical Composition.* 2 vol., New York, Associated Music Publishers, 1942.

RISSET, Jean-Claude, *An Introductory Catalogue of Computer Synthesized sounds,* Unpublished. Murray Hill, New Jersey, Bell Telephone Laboratories, 1969.

VON FOORSTER, Heinz and BEAUCHAMPS, James W., eds., *Music by Computers,* New York, John Wiley and sons, 1969.

SCHAEFFER, Pierre, *Traité des objets musicaux. Essais interdisciplines,* Paris, Éditions du Seuil, 1966.

MATHEWS, Max V., *The Technology of Computer Music,* Cambridge, M.I.T. Press, 1969.

FELLER, William, *An Introduction to Probability Theory and its Applications.* 2 vol., New York, John Wiley and sons, 1966.

POSTFACE

Mathematics, in Xenakis' music, plays an essential role as a philosophical catalyst, as a tool for the formal direction of sound or visual structures. Xenakis has also used computers in the composition of some if his scores. This musician who is also an architect, this man of science who is also a philosopher, has chosen the topic of "alloys" between the arts and sciences for his doctoral dissertation. Here we are publishing his defense of his dissertation complete with the jury's questions and interventions. It is not surprising that Olivier Messiaen has treated aspects of musical composition; Michel Ragon, aspects of architecture; and Michel Serres, aspects of mathematics and science. Summoned to explain himself and his music, Xenakis demonstrates that his culture is both philosophical and scientific, which is, as we all know, exceptional. Thus, we will become better acquainted with the man, about whom Antoine Golea has writteen "Xenakis is perhaps the most engaging, the most poignant and also the most provocative figure of twentieth century music." Let us also quote Claude Levi-Strauss who, when questioned on Xenakis by the *Quinzaine Litteraire*, responded, "I am very sensitive to his writings; I find them scholarly, intelligent, and subtle."